SPECIAL FORCES

Tales of Heroism from Around the World

STEVE STONE

Copy editing by Rachel Hunter

Contents

Foreword

Special Forces are highly revered and the soldiers themselves that are in these elite units have gone through a tough selection and training regime to make it onto the front line. Be it a Delta Force Operative, Navy SEAL, SAS Trooper or any other Special Forces operator. These individuals are the best of the best protecting not only their own countries, but people from many other countries as well. America like the British has nurtured and grown its Special Forces capability since the Second World War. America in particular, now has the largest Special Forces capability in the world.

Many spend a set period as a soldier before being eligible to apply for the chance to become part of the Special Forces community. Today, close collaboration is the key to many missions - even if the rivalry, to be the best, first to complete an objective or be the ones to take on a high-profile target such as Osama Bin Laden drives some operations. The stories in this book are chosen to show not only the success, but also the failure and lessons learnt from each and every operation. How close-knit teams have had to work hard to survive covering each other's backs in some horrific and almost overwhelming situations. High technology is still no replacement for boots on the ground, where highly trained operatives can still gather intelligence that no eye in the sky is capable of.

Special Forces as we know it, were born out of the Second World War; these elite units set the foundations. Before the SAS in World War Two, the Germans had their own elite unit at the start of the war in 1939. This was the prototype of the German force the Brandenburgers, which increased from a division to a battalion during the Second World War. Originally conceived by Hauptmann Todor von Hippel, who, after having his idea rejected approached Admiral Wilhelm Canaris, commander of the Abwehr, the German intelligence service. It led to the creation of a commando unit in the early years consisting of German expatriates fluent in other languages. They fought in most of Germany's campaigns. Smaller elements went to infiltrate Afghanistan, India, Middle Eastern countries and South Africa. They achieved great success during Germany's early campaigns by seizing strategic bridges, tunnels and marshalling yards in advance of the main German force. A typical operation would be to infiltrate a country in civilian clothing before the main German force launched its attack and seize strategic points. Along with the German Brandenburgers, the Italian's had their own small and highly successful elite force called the 10a Flottiglia MAS. They were a force of Italian frogmen from the Italian Navy. Their job was to attack allied shipping and performed many successful raids. Sometimes they used surface boats such as when HMS York was sunk by an explosive filled motor boat. During the war the 10a Flottigila MAS undertook more than 12 operations and sank or damaged five warships and 20 merchant ships.

Colonel Lucian K Truscott came to appreciate the British Commandos and raised via his superiors the need for a comparable US Army force. His concept paved the way for the US Army Rangers. The 1st Ranger Battalion first fought in northwest Africa and Italy. On the 29 January 1944 most of the 1st and 3rd Rangers were captured during the battle of Cisterna in central Italy. The greatest claim to fame for the Rangers came on 6 June 1944 with their attack on Pointe du Hoc during the D day invasion of France. The 2nd Ranger Battalion scaled a 150ft cliff, in order to destroy a six-gun battery. They were under constant fire during their climb up the cliff face. At the top the Rangers only encountered a small company of German soldiers. The artillery was withdrawn 500m further away before later being destroyed. The Rangers held the main road at Pointe du Hoc for two days before being relieved. The 6th Ranger Battalion led the US invasion of the Philippines and performed a daring raid at Cabanatuan, when they worked with Alamo Scouts and Filipino guerrillas to rescue 489 Allied prisoners of war as well as 33 civilians.

The camaraderie of being in the Armed Forces is something that has to be experienced to be fully appreciated, it becomes even more paramount in the small teams that Special Forces often operate. Sometimes spending weeks in close confines observing and waiting for the call to go into action miles behind enemy lines. It takes real mental toughness to be a Special Forces operative, being able to stay focused even when extreme fatigue is taking hold. A good example is the US Navy SEALs on Takur Ghar during Operation Anaconda. Taking on the overwhelming fire power of RPG and machine guns – relying solely on their superior training to survive and fight through even after sustaining injuries. The key point drilled in, during training is that if you let the fatigue take hold or give up, you will die; be it due to the climate or due to the enemy getting the better of you. Special Forces are just that 'Special' they need to be one step ahead of the enemy, even a highly trained or battle-hardened enemy such as the Taliban.

The face of war has changed and with that, Special Forces have become more and more a necessity, not only taking the fight to the enemy stronghold, but protecting our towns and cities. The new threat from what is called 'marauding terrorist firearms attack' has already been seen in shopping malls and other public places across the globe. When an AK-47 can be bought for as little as 30 dollars in some African nations - a weapon that can go through a brick wall, even a double skinned brick wall like a knife through butter. It is not hard to think what devastation it can cause, if unleashed in a crowded area such as a shopping mall or busy streets. The lone wolf terrorist who decides almost on a whim to go on a marauding attack be it with a gun or some form explosive. Often these have become indoctrinated and made to believe that by performing such atrocious attacks will lead to some form of spiritual redemption.

Special Forces along with their intelligence services are monitoring the various threats across the globe on covert operations. The more proactive missions are still being undertaken in Afghanistan, Syria and Libya; although unconfirmed in Syria. The setting up of E Squadron, 22 SAS in 2005 to enable a closer working relationship with Mi6 shows the growing relationship with the intelligence community and Special Forces. SEAL Team Six was also born out of the need for a more specialist unit to deal with terrorism. The same brief led to the inception of Delta Force under Charles Beckwith.

This collection of stories from across the globe gives a good historical account of a wide variety of operations and opponents over the past 35 years. The technology has moved on but the tactics and the nuts and bolts of an operation has changed very little.

Special Forces, in terms of the wider military history, have not been with us that long. Small teams in various wars over the centuries have been put in place to carry out specific tasks, and you could think of these loosely as Special Forces. The Chinese strategist Jiang Ziya, in his Six Secret Teachings, describes recruiting talented and highly-motivated men for serving in specialised elite units where they would undertake tasks, such as making rapid long-distance advances. In the late Roman period,

Roman fleets used small, fast camouflaged ships that were crewed by selected men for commando and scouting missions.

In many ways, though, the implementation of Special Forces over the last century has been done in an almost stop-start fashion as military planners have slowly figured out how to best utilise them, both in warfare and peace time. The SBS came first, in mid-1940, initially as the Special Boat Section and later became the Special Boat Squadron, before becoming the Special Boat Service in 1987. The SAS was in essence the first and arguably most famous of the Special Forces units. The SAS (Special Air Service) was borne out of an idea by David Stirling in 1941 and his experience with commando units. In World War II, 1SBS became attached to the SAS before both the SAS and SBS were disbanded after the war. The SBS role was integrated within the Royal Marine Commandos, as was the title. The Special Boat Squadron name was not used until 1977. The SAS re-emerged initially as a Territorial unit before becoming 22 SAS and added to the army list in 1952.

The US Navy Seals can also trace their roots back to World War II, when the United States Navy saw the need for the covert reconnaissance of the landing beaches and coastal defences. This led to the formation of the Amphibious Scout and Raider School in 1942. The Navy knew it needed to determine the role of its Special Forces, which prompted Arleigh Burke, Chief of Naval Operations in March 1961, to recommend the establishment of guerrilla and counter-guerrilla units. These units would be able to operate from sea, air or land. This was the beginning of the Navy SEALs as they are known today. Following this was John F. Kennedy's pledge of $100 million, put in place to strengthen U.S. Special Forces.

Delta Force is one of the newer Special Forces Units. Thoughts about setting up Delta Force date back to the 1960s, although it was the various terrorist actions and threats during the 1970s that led to its fruition in 1977. Colonel Charles Beckwith after seeing the SAS in action realised that the U.S. Army needed a similar force. The SAS was invited to help train the initial recruits for Delta Force, as Delta Force was based on the SAS in many ways. Delta Force has grown to be one of the largest and most well-equipped Special Forces units in the world. Many other countries have their own Special Forces, as the ever-changing world in which we live has had to respond to terrorist attacks and the changing face of war. This has determined the demand for small, specialised groups of highly-trained personnel to counter the threats various countries have faced, as well as in support of other countries across the globe. The Special Force personnel are the elite in many of the world's armies and are comprised of the best of the best, with rigorous selection and training programs.

This book looks at some of the key missions and operations undertaken by Special Forces around the world. Not all have been successful but have been key in the implementation of changes. Changes that have given rise to better command, tactics and equipment - to give Special Forces on the ground the best chance possible of executing a successful operation. But nothing can be taken away from the bravery and gallantry shown by Special Forces even under great adversity and in more recent time's political changes, which has defined both their composition and operations. The SAS uses the motto 'Who Dares Wins' and that motto is true of all Special Forces in reality. As they all undertake daring missions and push through to win, sometimes against overwhelming odds. Sometimes paying with their lives as some of the true stories in this book show.

Battle of Mirbat

Mirbat is a small town on the southwestern coast of Oman. Britain had assisted the Omani government by sending elements of the SAS to both train soldiers and also win against the Popular Front for the Liberation of the Occupied Arabian Gulf (PFLOAG) guerrillas to win the "hearts and minds" of the Omani people.

At 0600 hours on 19 July 1972, the PFLOAG attacked the British Army Training Team (BATT) house, which housed nine SAS soldiers, the house was situated just outside the Port of Mirbat. The PFLOAG (known by the locals as the Adoo) attacked the SAS BATT house knowing that in order to reach the Port of Mirbat, they would first have to defeat the SAS guarding the approach to the town in Jebel Ali, a series of small desert slopes leading to the Port. That gave any defending force a tactical advantage.

The OIC (Officer in Command), Captain Mike Kealy observed the waves of Adoo advancing on the fort, but did not order his men to open fire because he thought it was a group of Omani Army coming in for the night shift. Who were positioned on the slopes to give advance warning of any approaching Adoo. However, it was soon realised by Kealy that this was an attack and the Omani Army lookouts had all been killed.

Kealy ordered his men to open fire. The men took up various positions behind the sandbag parapet on the roof of the BATT house, firing at the Adoo with L1A1 SLR battle rifles. The SLR rifle was the standard British Army rifle before being replaced by the SA80 in the mid-1980s. Another member of the SAS team was firing a Browning M2HB heavy machine gun, firing .50 calibre rounds used extensively since the 1930s for vehicle, boat and aircraft armament. A further two SAS troopers were on the ground level operating a mortar protected by sandbags. The Adoo had AK47s and also mortars that were being used quite effectively around the BATT house.

With a further two men on ground level, operating and firing an infantry mortar surrounded by sandbags. The Adoo were armed with AK-47 assault rifles, and were mortar bombing the area around the BATT house. Kealy ordered the signaller to get in contact with SAS Headquarters at Um al Quarif, to request reinforcements. A small number of Omani Intelligence Service personnel in the BATT House, a small contingent of Pakistani soldiers and a member of British Military Intelligence Corporal.

The Pakistani did not want to join in initially, but were ordered to by Kealy. At the current range the SLR was not effective against the Adoo until they got closer at just under 2000 feet. Other than the Browning and the mortar, the SAS had no other effective weapons. Sergeant Talaiasi Labalaba made a run for the 25 Pounder Artillery Piece which was positioned next to a smaller fort, which stationed nine Omani Army Special Forces soldiers, who had not played a part in the battle so far.

The Omani policeman who was guarding the 25 Pounder had been seriously wounded. Labalaba managed to operate the weapon, which is a six-man job, himself and fire a round a minute at the approaching Adoo, directing their attention away from the BATT house. Kealy received a radio message from Labalaba reporting that a bullet had skimmed his face, and he was badly injured. He was struggling to operate the gun by himself, so Kealy asked for a volunteer to run to Talaiasi's aid. Trooper Sekonaia Takavesi volunteered to run the gauntlet of fire to the 25 Pounder to aid Labalaba. As Takavesi ran, the rest of the SAS troopers in the BATT house provided covering fire as he ran the 800 metres dodging bullets impacting the ground all around him. Initially, Takavesi tried to give aid to his injured friend, while firing at the approaching Adoo with his personal weapon.

Realising that they needed help, Takavesi tried to raise the small number of Omani soldiers inside the smaller fort, and Walid Khamis emerged. The only Omani Gendarmerie Officer in the Mirbat Fort was Lieutenant Hassan Bin Ehsan Bin Naseeb. The remaining Omani soldiers in the fort engaged the enemy with small arms fire from firing positions on the roof and through the windows of the fort, trying to hold back the Adoo. As the two men made it back to the emplacement, an Omani soldier fell wounded after being shot in the stomach with a 7.62 mm bullet. The Adoo continued to advance upon the BATT house, and artillery emplacement. At one point, the Adoo were so close Labalaba and Takavesi fired the weapon at point blank range, aiming down the barrel. Labalaba crawled across a small space to reach the 60 mm Infantry Mortar, but fell dead after being shot in the neck. Takavesi, was shot through the shoulder and grazed by a bullet to the back of his head, but he continued to fire at the approaching Adoo with his personal weapon. The signaller back at the BATT house sent messages through to the main Forward Operating Base, to request air support and medical evacuation for the men in the gun emplacement. The situation was becoming more and more desperate. Kealy and Trooper Tobin made a run to the artillery piece. Upon reaching it, they dived in to avoid increasingly intense gunfire from the Adoo. Takavesi continued to fire on the attackers, propped up against sand bags after being shot through the stomach, with the bullet narrowly missing his spine. The Adoo threw several hand grenades, but only one detonated, exploding behind the gun emplacement with no one injured. During the battle, Trooper Tobin attempted to reach over the body of Labalaba. In so doing, Tobin was mortally wounded when a bullet struck his face. By this time, BAC Strikemaster light-attack jets of the Sultan of Oman's Air Force had arrived on scene and began strafing the Adoo in the Jebel Ali. With a low cloud base, making for low altitude attack runs, only machine-guns and light rockets were used. Reinforcements arrived from SAS G Squadron, and defeated the Adoo, the Adoo withdrew at about 0030 hours. All the wounded SAS soldiers were evacuated, and given medical treatment, Trooper Tobin eventually died in hospital not due to the multiple gunshot wounds, but due to an infection in his lung, caused by a splintered tooth which he had breathed in, when his bottom jaw was blown off by an AK47 round.

The 25-pounder gun, which is now known as the "Mirbat gun" used very effectively by Labalaba during the siege, is now housed in the Firepower Museum of the Royal Artillery at the former Royal Arsenal, Woolwich. Though killed in action, Labalaba displayed remarkable bravery by single-handedly operating the 25-pounder gun, a weapon normally requiring four to six soldiers to operate. Labalaba's heroism was a key factor in halting the Adoo's vicious assault on the emplacement, allowing time for reinforcements to arrive. Labalaba was awarded a posthumous Mention in Dispatches for his actions in the Battle of Mirbat, though some of his comrades have since campaigned for him to be awarded the more prestigious Victoria Cross. Kealy received the Distinguished Service Order, Takavesi the Distinguished Conduct Medal for their part in the battle. The Battle of Mirbat has gone down in SAS history and demonstrates, how nine highly trained and determined SAS soldiers were able to hold back, a far numerically superior force of around 300 Adoo until reinforcements arrived. Ultimately, killing over 80 of the 300 Adoo.

Operation Entebbe - Mossad

Operation Entebbe, which had the military codename 'Operation Thunderbolt,' was put in place after the hijacking of a civilian airliner. The operation took place at night. With Israeli transport planes carrying 100 commandos over 2,500 miles to Uganda for the rescue operation. Uganda is a landlocked country in East Africa. It gained independence from Britain on 9 October 1962. After a military coup in 1971, Milton Obote the executive Prime Minister was deposed from power and the dictator Idi Amin seized control of the country. Amin ruled Uganda with the military for the next eight years and carried out mass killings within the country to maintain his rule. An estimated 300,000 Ugandans lost their lives at the hands of his regime, many of them in the north, which he associated with Obote's loyalists.

On 27 June 1976, Air France Flight 139, an Airbus A300 (Airbus A300B4-203), registration F-BVG, which had flown from Tel Aviv, Israel, carrying 246 passengers and a crew of 12. An additional 58 passengers, including the four hijackers, waited to board at the Athens airport in Greece, before the plane heading for Paris. Not long after the plane took off at 1230 hours, the flight was hijacked by two Palestinians from the Popular Front for the Liberation of Palestine – External Operations (PFLP-EO), along with two Germans, Wilfried Böse and Brigitte Kuhlmann, from the German Revolutionary Cells of the PFLP. Once the hijackers had taken over the plane, they ordered by the pilot to divert the flight to Benghazi, Libya. On landing in Libya, it was held on the ground for seven hours to refuel. Whilst on the ground the hijackers released a female hostage who pretended to have a miscarriage. The plane left Benghazi, and headed towards Uganda. The plane landed at Entebbe Airport at around 1515 hours on the 28 June, over 24 hours after the flight's original departure.

Four supporters from the pro-Palestinian forces of Uganda's President, Idi Amin joined the four original hijackers at Entebbe. They released their demands, which was for the immediate release of 40 Palestinians held in Israel and 13 other detainees imprisoned in Kenya, France, Switzerland, and West Germany. If their demands were not met, they would begin killing hostages from 1 July 1976.

The hostages were put into groups by the hijackers, Jews and Israelis as one group and everyone else in another. All the passengers were taken to the transit hall of Entebbe. Some of the passengers were released, leaving 106 remaining as hostages. As the crisis unfolded, attempts were made to negotiate the release of the hostages. The Egyptian government under Sadat tried to negotiate with both the PLO and the Ugandan government, and special envoy Hanni al Hassan was sent to negotiate in Uganda.

The hijackers announced that the airline crew and non-Jewish passengers would be released and put on another Air France plane brought to Entebbe for that purpose. The captain of the original, hijacked Air France flight, Michel Bacos, told the hijackers that all passengers, including those who remained, were his responsibility and that he would not leave them behind. Bacos's entire crew followed suit. A French nun also refused to leave, insisting that one of the remaining hostages take her place, but Ugandan soldiers forced her into the waiting Air France plane. A total of 85 Israeli and non-Israeli Jewish hostages remained, plus another 20, 12 of whom were the crew of the Air France plane.

President Idi Amin allowed several more Palestinians to join the original hijackers. When the Israeli authorities failed to negotiate a political solution, they decided the only option was a military operation to rescue the hostages. In the week before the raid, Israel tried a number of political avenues to try to obtain the release of the hostages. Some within the Israeli cabinet, felt that if a military operation was not successful Palestinian prisoners should be released. Phone negotiations with Idi Amin were unsuccessful. The Israeli government also approached the US government to deliver a message to Egyptian president Anwar Sadat, asking him to request Amin to release the hostages. On 1 July 1976 deadline, the Israeli government needed to extend the deadline to give more time, for the military operation to be put in place. The Israeli government got the deadline extended to 4 July. On 3 July at 1830 hours, the Israeli cabinet approved the rescue mission. Brig. Gen Shomron was appointed as the operation commander. Whilst planning the raid, the Israeli forces had to figure out how to refuel the Lockheed C-130 Hercules aircraft they intended to use while en route to Entebbe. The Israelis lacked the logistical capacity to aerially refuel four to six aircraft so far from Israeli airspace. While several East African nations, including the logistically preferred choice Kenya, were sympathetic, none wished to incur the wrath of Amin or the Palestinians by allowing the Israelis to land their aircraft within their borders to refuel.

However, the raid would not be able to be undertaken without assistance from at least one East African government. It was the Kenyan government who was finally persuaded to support the Israeli operation. It was most likely pressure from the Jewish community within Kenya along with the Israeli community that aided in the decision.

The IDF task force was now allowed, not only to cross Kenyan airspace and refuel at the Jomo Kenyatta International Airport. Kenyan Minister of Agriculture Bruce MacKenzie persuaded Kenyan President Kenyatta to permit Israeli Mossad agents to gather information before the hostage rescue operation in Uganda, and to allow Israeli Air Force aircraft to land and refuel at a Nairobi airport after the rescue. However, MacKenzie would pay the ultimate price for his actions, as Idi Amin ordered Ugandan agents to assassinate him. On 24 May 1978, he was killed when a time bomb was attached to his plane and exploded midair over Ngong Hill in Kenya, after it had taken off from Entebbe Airport in Uganda.

Mossad built an accurate picture of the whereabouts of the hostages, the number of terrorists, and the involvement of Ugandan troops from the released hostages in Paris.

Solel Boneh, a large Israeli construction company that had built the terminal where the hostages were held. Was consulted on the layout, so a partial replica could be constructed to aid in the training of the IDF. After Betzer collected intelligence and planned for several days, four Israeli Air Force C-130 Hercules transport aircraft secretly flew to Entebbe Airport at midnight without being detected by Entebbe air traffic control. Taking off from Sharm al-Sheikh Airport, Egypt, the task force flew down the international flight path over the Red Sea, mostly flying at a height of no more than 30 m (100 ft) to avoid radar detection by Egyptian, Sudanese, and Saudi Arabian forces. Near the southern outlet of the Red Sea the C-130s turned south and passed south of Djibouti. From there, they went to a point northeast of Nairobi, Kenya, likely across Somalia and the Ogaden area of Ethiopia. They turned west, passing through the African Rift Valley and over Lake Victoria. Two Boeing 707 jets followed the cargo planes. The first 707 contained medical facilities and landed at Jomo Kenyatta International Airport in Nairobi, Kenya. The commander of the operation, General Yekutiel Adam, was on board the second Boeing, which circled over Entebbe Airport during the raid.

The Israeli ground task force numbered approximately 100 personnel. A 29-man assault unit led by Lt. Col. Yonatan Netanyahu, this force was composed entirely of commandos from Sayeret Matkal, and was given the primary task of assaulting the old terminal and rescuing the hostages. Israeli forces, finally landed at Entebbe Airport at 2300 hours, with their cargo bay doors already open. A black Mercedes that looked like President Idi Amin's vehicle and Land Rovers that usually accompanied Amin's Mercedes were brought along. The Israelis hoped they could use them to bypass security checkpoints. When the C-130s landed, Israeli assault team members drove the vehicles to the terminal building in the same fashion as Amin. As they approached the terminal, two Ugandan sentries, who knew that Idi Amin had recently purchased a white Mercedes, ordered the vehicles to stop. With no other alternative, the commandos shot the sentries using silenced pistols, but did not kill them. As they pulled away, an Israeli commando in one of the following Land Rovers killed them with an unsuppressed rifle. Fearing the hijackers would be alerted prematurely, by the noise of a rifle, the assault team quickly approached the terminal.

The Commandos sprang from their vehicles and hurried towards the terminal. The hostages were in the main hall of the airport building, directly adjacent to the runway. Entering the terminal, the commandos shouted through a megaphone, "Stay down! Stay down! We are Israeli soldiers," in both Hebrew and English. Jean-Jacques Maimoni, a 19-year-old French immigrant to Israel who chose to identify himself as an Israeli Jew to the hijackers even though he also had a French passport— stood up and was killed, when Israeli company commander Muki Betzer and another soldier mistook him for a hijacker and fired at him. Another hostage, Pasco Cohen, 52, the manager of an Israeli medical insurance fund, was also fatally wounded by gunfire from the commandos. In addition, a third hostage, 56-year-old Ida Borochovitch, a Russian Jew who had immigrated to Israel, was also killed in the crossfire.

Wilfried Böse was the only hijacker who entered the hall housing the hostages after the rescue mission had begun. At first, he pointed his AK-47 rifle at the hostages, but thought better of that idea and ordered them to find shelter in the restroom. Instead he opened up on the Commandos before being killed by fire from them.

At one point, an Israeli commando called out in Hebrew, "Where are the rest of them?" referring to the hijackers. The hostages pointed to a connecting door of the airport's main hall, into which the commandos threw several hand grenades. They entered the room and shot dead the three remaining hijackers, ending the assault. Meanwhile, the other three C-130 Hercules had landed and unloaded armoured personnel carriers to provide defence during the anticipated hour needed to refuel. These were also used to destroy Ugandan MiG fighter planes on the ground, to prevent them from pursuing, as the force made good their escape. After the rescue mission, the commandos returned to their aircraft and began loading the hostages. Ugandan soldiers shot at them as they tried to get the hostages on board. The commandos returned fire with their AK-47s, inflicting casualties on the Ugandans. During this brief but intense firefight, Ugandan soldiers fired from the Airport control tower. Israeli commander Yonatan Netanyahu was shot in the chest and killed, possibly by a Ugandan sniper. He was the only Israeli commando killed in the operation. At least five other commandos were wounded during the firefight. Commandos fired light machine guns and an RPG back at the control tower, suppressing the Ugandans' fire. The commandos finished evacuating the hostages, picked up and loaded Netanyahu's body into one of the planes, and left Entebbe Airport.

The entire operation had lasted 53 minutes - of which the assault lasted only 30 minutes. All seven hijackers present, and it is thought between 33 and 45 Ugandan soldiers were killed during the operation. About 11 Ugandan Army Air Force MiG-17 fighter planes were destroyed on the ground as well. Out of the 106 hostages, three were killed, one was left in Uganda, and approximately 10 were wounded. The 102 rescued hostages were flown to Israel via Nairobi, Kenya, shortly after the raid. To this very day, bullet holes from the firefight are still clearly visible on the terminal building. Outraged by the raid Idi Amin organised that the Norfolk hotel, owned by the Block Hotels who owner had influenced the Kenyan government about helping Israel, was bombed on 31

December 1980 by the PFLP/PLO. The attack, in which 13 people of several nationalities were killed and 87 more were wounded. The bombing was the first act of foreign terrorism perpetrated on Kenyan soil.

Al-Sa'iqa Unit Larnaca Disaster

In the late hours of 18 February 1978, Youssef Sebai, editor of a prominent Egyptian newspaper and a friend of the Egyptian President, Anwar Sadat, was assassinated by two Palestinian gunmen at a convention being held at the Nicosia Hilton in Cyprus. The two assassins rounded up 16 Arab convention delegates as hostages with two of them being P.L.O. representatives and an Egyptian national. They demanded transportation to Larnaca International Airport. At the airport waiting for them should be a Cyprus Airways DC-8 aircraft. Following negotiations with the Cypriot authorities, the hijackers were allowed to fly the aircraft out of Cyprus with 11 hostages and four crew members aboard. The aircraft, however, was denied permission to land in Djibouti, Syria and Saudi Arabia. This meant the hijackers had no choice but to return and land in Cyprus a few hours after they had left Cyprus.

The Egyptian President Anwar Sadat, was aggrieved by the assassination of his personal friend and begged the Cypriot President, Spyros Kyprianou to rescue the hostages and extradite the terrorists to Cairo. The Cypriot President responded by promising to oversee the rescue operation and any negotiations personally, and travelled to the airport himself. Sadat decided to dispatch an elite anti-terrorism unit (Task Force 777) to Cyprus aboard a C-130 Hercules transport aircraft. Cairo merely informed Kyprianou that "people are on the way to help rescue the hostages" and did not reveal who was on board nor what their intentions were. Upon landing in Cyprus, the Egyptian force immediately launched an all-out assault, dispatching a single Jeep with three men to race ahead of an estimated between 58 and 75 troops, which moved towards the hijacked aircraft on foot.

As the Egyptian Special Forces advanced quickly towards the hijacked DC-8 aircraft and the Cypriot National Guard forces who surrounded it, the Cypriot forces reportedly issued a single verbal warning to halt and submit, though in other reports, the Cypriots issued two verbal warnings, the second a demand for the Egyptians to return to their aircraft. As this occurred, the occupants of the Jeep and the Cypriot National Guardsmen exchanged gunfire, and the Egyptian Jeep was struck by a RPG as well as gunfire, killing all three occupants. As the vehicle came to a halt, the Cypriots and the main Egyptian force confronted each other at a range of less than 300 metres, and it is variously reported that the

Egyptians, who lacked any form of cover, dropped down onto the tarmac in prone firing positions. At this moment, the two forces engaged each other with heavy gunfire, and the Cypriots opened fire on the Egyptian C-130H aircraft with a 106 mm anti-tank missile, striking it in the nose and killing all three crew on board. With the C-130 destroyed, the Egyptian force and the Cypriot National Guard exchanged heavy gunfire for nearly an hour in sporadic fighting on the open tarmac. Some of the Egyptian troops took cover in a nearby empty Air France aircraft.

Cypriot President Spyros Kyprianou, who was watching the events unfolding from the airport control tower, was forced to withdraw from the windows and take cover as Egyptian commandos struck the tower with automatic gunfire. When the firefight finally subsided, 12 Egyptian Special Forces were killed as well as the aircrew of the Egyptian C-130. A further 15 Special Forces commandos were taken to hospital with gunshot wounds. The Cypriots suffered no casualties, mainly due to having suitable cover to fire from.

After the failed attack, the Egyptians found out that the surrender of the hostages had already been arranged at the time of the failed attack being launched. The two terrorists were later extradited to Egypt to stand trial. After the trial they both received death sentences, which was later changed to life sentences. On 20 February 1978, Eygpt recalled its diplomatic mission and requested that Cyprus do the same. Egypt and Cyprus severed political ties until the assassination of Sadat. Sadat was assassinated on 6 October 1981 during the annual victory parade held in Cairo to celebrate Operation Badr. Sadat was protected by four layers of security and eight bodyguards, and the army parade should have been safe due to ammunition-seizure rules.

As Egyptian Air Force Mirage jets flew overhead, distracting the crowd, Egyptian Army soldiers and troop trucks towing artillery paraded by. One truck contained the assassination squad, led by Lieutenant Khalid Islambouli. As it passed the tribune, Islambouli forced the driver at gunpoint to stop. From there, the assassins dismounted and Islambouli approached Sadat with three hand grenades concealed under his helmet. Sadat stood to receive his salute, whereupon, Islambouli threw all his grenades at Sadat, only one of which exploded, but fell short. Additional assassins rose from the truck, indiscriminately firing AK-47 assault rifles into the stands. After Sadat was hit and fell to the ground, people threw chairs around him to shield him from the hail of bullets. In total the attack lasted about two minutes. Sadat and eleven others were killed outright or suffered fatal wounds. Islambouli and the other assassins were tried, found guilty, sentenced to death, and executed by firing squad in April 1982. A year after the disastrous attack, Unit 777 was established as Eygpts elite anti-terrorist and special forces unit.

Operation Feuerzauber

At 1100 hours on October 13, 1977, Lufthansa flight LH 181, a Boeing 737, took off from Palma de Mallorca, Majorca and due to fly to Frankfurt, Germany with 86 passengers and 5 crew, piloted by Jürgen Schumann, with co-pilot Jürgen Vietor at the controls. About 30 minutes into the flight as it passed over Marseilles, France, the aircraft was hijacked by four militants calling themselves "Commando Martyr Halime." Their leader was a 2-year-old Palestinian named Zohair Youssif Akache, who adopted the alias "Captain Martyr Mahmud". The other three were 22-year-old Suhaila Sayeh a Palestinian, 23-year-old Wabil Harb and 22-year-old Hind Alameh who were both Lebanese. Akache burst into the cockpit with a loaded pistol in his hand and ordered Vietor to join the passengers, leaving Schumann to take over the flight controls. Akache ordered Schumann to fly to Larnaca in Cyprus but was told that they had insufficient fuel and would have to land in Rome first.

The aircraft changed course and landed in Rome, Italy, for refuelling. Acting with the Red Army Faction group, the Siegfried Hausner Commando, who had kidnapped West German industrialist Hanns Martin Schleyer 5 weeks earlier, demanded the release of ten RAF (Red Army Faction) terrorists detained at the JVA Stuttgart-Stammheim prison plus two Palestinian compatriots held in Turkey and $15 million US dollars. German Interior Minister Werner Maihofer contacted his Italian counterpart Francesco Cossiga and made the suggestion that the plane's tires should be shot out to prevent the aircraft from leaving. After consulting his colleagues Cossiga decided that the most desirable solution for the Italian government was to get rid of the problem altogether. The aircraft was refuelled, which enabled Akache to instruct Vietor to take off for Larnaca at 1745 hours after being allowed back into the cockpit on the ground, without obtaining clearance from Rome air traffic control.

The plane flew to and landed in Larnaca, Cyprus, at 2028 hours. After about an hour, a local PLO representative arrived at the airport and over the radio tried to persuade Akache to release the hostages. This led to a furious response from Akache who became quite animated as he screamed in Arabic over the intercom and the PLO representative had to give up. The plane was refuelled and Schumann asked flight control for a routing to Beirut. He was told that Beirut airport was blocked and closed to them and Akache told Schumann that they would go to Damascus instead. The plane took off at 2250 hours still heading to Beirut, but was refused landing permission. After also being denied landing permission in Syria, Damascus, Iraq, Baghdad and Kuwait they headed for Bahrain.

Schumann was told by a passing Qantas airliner that Bahrain airport was closed. He radioed flight control and told them they had insufficient fuel to go elsewhere and despite being told again that the airport was closed, Schumann was suddenly given an automatic landing frequency by the flight controller. They finally landed in Bahrain at 0152 hours the following morning. On arrival, almost as soon as the aircraft came to a standstill, it was surrounded by armed troops. On seeing troops surround the aircraft, Akache radioed the tower and said that unless the troops were withdrawn, he would shoot the co-pilot. After a standoff with the tower, with Akache setting a 5-minute deadline and holding a pistol to Vietor's head, the troops were withdrawn. The aircraft was refuelled and they took off for Dubai.

As the plane approached Dubai, where they were again refused landing permission. As the plane overflew the airport in the early light of dawn, it was easy to see that the runway had been blocked with trucks and fire engines. Running short of fuel Schumann told the tower they would have to land anyway. As they made a low pass over the airport, they saw that various obstacles placed on the runway were being removed. At 0540 hours on 14 October 1977, Vietor was able to make a normal landing on the main runway.

Once the plane had taxied off the runway and come to a stop, the terrorists asked the tower to supply water, food, medicine and newspapers, and to take away the garbage. Captain Jürgen Schumann was able to communicate the number of hijackers on board. In a press conference this information was revealed by Dubai's Sheikh Mohammed, Minister of Defence. The hijackers learned about this, causing Akache to go into another rage and threaten to kill Schumann. The aircraft remained on the ground at Dubai all through that day and night. The following morning Akache threatened to start shooting hostages if the aircraft was not refuelled and the Dubai authorities finally agreed. In the meantime, both Hans-Jürgen Wischnewski, the West German minister responsible for handling the hijacking, and Colonel Ulrich Wegener, commander of the elite German anti-terrorist squad GSG 9, had arrived in Dubai to try to get the government to agree to let GSG 9 commandos into Dubai to storm the aircraft and rescue the hostages.

On September 5, 1972, the Palestinian terrorist movement Black September infiltrated the Summer Olympic Games in Munich, West Germany, to kidnap 11 Israeli athletes, killing 2 in the Olympic Village during the initial assault on the athletes' rooms. The incident escalated when German police, neither trained nor equipped for counterterrorism operations, and underestimating the number of terrorists involved, attempted to rescue the athletes. They failed in their attempt to mount a rescue operation with one police officer killed and five out of the eight kidnappers along with all of the remaining nine hostages. Apart from the human tragedy, Germany's law enforcement found itself severely compromised, in part due to its historic relationship to Jews and Israel.

As a consequence of the mismanagement of the Olympic tragedy, the West German government created the GSG 9 under the leadership of then Oberstleutnant Ulrich Wegener so that similar situations in the future could be responded to adequately and professionally. Many German politicians opposed its formation, fearing GSG 9 would rekindle memories of the Nazi Party's Schutzstaffel (SS). The decision was taken to form the unit from police forces as opposed to the military as was the model that other countries had chosen. On the grounds that German federal law expressly forbids the use of the military forces against the civilian population. Special Forces composed of police personnel would overcome this. The unit was officially established on April 17, 1973 as a part of Germany's federal police agency, the Bundesgrenzschutz (Federal Border Guard Service, renamed Bundespolizei or Federal Police in 2005). The name GSG 9 stood for Grenzschutzgruppe 9 (Border Guard Group 9) and was chosen simply because the BGS had eight regular border guard groups at the time. After the 2005 renaming, the abbreviation "GSG 9" was kept due to the fame of the unit and is now the official way to refer to the unit. Its formation was based on the expertise of the Israeli Sayeret Matkal.

After permission was granted by the Dubi government for GSG 9 commandos to storm the aircraft, SAS and GSG 9 senior operatives insisted on additional combat exercise and dry-runs on an adjacent airstrip. Around 45 hours of supplementary training was conducted whilst based in Dubai. While Wegener was considering his options, the plane had completed its refuelling and at 12:20 am on 17 October 1977, it took off, heading for Salalah, Oman, where landing permission was once again denied. A course to Aden, South Yemen, at the limit of their fuel range, was set.

In Aden, South Yemen, they were again denied landing permission and the two main runways were blocked by vehicles. The plane was running low on fuel so Vietor had no choice but to make an emergency landing on a sand strip almost parallel to both runways. The Aden authorities told the hijackers that they would have to leave, but the two pilots were unsure over the condition of the plane after an emergency landing on sandy ground. Akache consequently gave Schumann permission to leave the aircraft in order to check the condition of the landing gear following the rough landing, and the engines. However, Schumann did not immediately return to the plane after the inspection, even after numerous attempts to recall him or even a threat to blow up the aircraft on the ground. To this day, the reasons for his long absence are unknown, but he may have been trying to alert authorities.

After this Schumann returned to the aircraft to face the wrath of Akache and his fiery temper, who forced him to kneel on the floor in the passenger cabin and shot him in the head without giving him a chance to explain himself. The plane was refueled at 0600 hours on 17 October co-pilot Jürgen Vietor, attempted to get in the air from the sandy runway. The plane slowly and laboriously picked up speed before taking off from Aden on course for the Somali capital of Mogadishu.

At around 0622 hour's local time, the plane made an unannounced and perfect landing in Mogadishu, Somalia. Akache told Vietor that he had provided a super-human performance and that he was consequently free to leave the aircraft since they were not planning to fly elsewhere. However, Vietor opted to remain on board with passengers and the rest of the crew. Schumann's body was thrown on the tarmac along with an ultimatum, which was for the RAF prisoners to be released by 1600 hours local time or the aircraft would be blown up. After pouring the duty-free spirits over the hostages in preparation for the destruction of the aircraft, the hijackers were told that the West German government had agreed to release the RAF prisoners, but told Akache that their transfer to Mogadishu would take several more hours, so Akache agreed to extend the deadline to 0230 hours on the 18 October.

Meantime, while the West German Chancellor Helmut Schmidt was attempting to negotiate an agreement with Somali President Siad Barre, special envoy Hans-Jürgen Wischnewski and GSG 9 commander Ulrich Wegener arrived at Mogadishu airport from Jeddah in a Lufthansa aircraft co-piloted by Rüdiger von Lutzau. In West Germany, a team of 30 GSG 9 commandos under their deputy commander, Major Klaus Blatte had assembled at Hangelar airfield near Bonn awaiting instructions. The commandos took off from Cologne-Bonn Airport on a Boeing 707 on 17 October to fly to nearby Djibouti while Schmidt negotiated with the Somalis. When they were flying over Ethiopia, agreement was reached and permission was given to land at Mogadishu. The Boeing 707 landed at 2000 hours local time with all lights out to avoid detection by the hijackers.

It took four hours to unload all of their equipment and to undertake the necessary reconnaissance, Wegener and Blatte finalised the assault plan, scheduled to start at 0200 hours local time. They had decided to approach from the rear of the aircraft in its blind spot in six teams. Using black-painted aluminium ladders to gain access to the aircraft through the escape hatches under the fuselage and via the doors over the wings. In the meantime, a fictitious progress report on the journey being taken by the released prisoners was being fed to Akache, by the German representatives in the airport tower. Just after 0200 hours, Akache was told that the plane carrying the prisoners had just departed Cairo after refuelling and he was asked to provide the conditions of the prisoner/hostage exchange over the radio.

Several minutes before the rescue, Somali soldiers lit a large fire 200 feet in front of the jet, as a diversionary tactic, prompting Akache and two of the three hijackers to rush to the cockpit and isolating them from the hostages in the cabin. This meant that GSG 9 knew their locality and would also help in reducing the possibility of casualties caused by friendly fire or hostages caught in the crossfire.

At 0207 hours local time, the GSG 9 commandos silently climbed up the blackened aluminium ladders and slowly opened the emergency doors, ensuring they made as little noise a possible. Wegener, at the head of one group, opened the forward door, and two other groups, led by Sergeant-Major Dieter Fox and Sergeant Joachim Huemmer stormed the aircraft by using the ladders to climb up onto the wings and opened both emergency doors at the same time. Shouting in German for the passengers and crew to hit the floor, the commandos shot and killed two of the terrorists, Wabil Harb and Hind Alameh, wounded Zohair Akache and Suhaila Sayeh, who was hiding in the toilet. Akache died of his injury's hours later. Three passengers and a flight attendant were slightly wounded. An American passenger aboard the plane later described the rescue. "I saw the door open and a man appears. His face was painted black and he starts shouting in German 'We're here to rescue you, get down! They started shooting."

There are still some rumours over whether members of the British SAS were directly involved in the operation. During an interview in 2007, GSG 9 Commander Ulrich Wegener stated that two SAS members were in Dubai as observers and made suggestions, but beyond that, weren't involved in the operation. The SAS had proposed to board the aircraft through only one entrance while GSG 9 strategy was to board through all available entrances. The SAS offered a type of new flash/stun grenades later to be used during the Iranian Embassy hostage rescue in 1980. GSG 9 did have a go at using them, but after several tests they were rejected as their high phosphor portion would have dramatically increased the danger of a fire inside the cabin. At the time airline interiors still had highly flammable seat foam and some interior fittings.

With all the hijackers taken out, the emergency escape chutes were deployed and passengers and crew were ordered to quickly evacuate the aircraft. At 0212 hours local time, just five minutes after the assault had commenced, the commandos radioed: "Frühlingszeit! Frühlingszeit!" ("Springtime! Springtime!"), which was the code word for the successful completion of the operation. A few moments later a radio signal was sent to Chancellor Schmidt in Bonn: Four opponents down – hostages free – four hostages slightly wounded – one commando slightly wounded.

The GSG 9 team escorted all 86 passengers to safety, and a few hours later they were all flown to Cologne-Bonn Airport, where they landed in the early afternoon of Tuesday 18 October, and were given a hero's welcome. In total 30 GSG 9 operators along with 2 SAS observers were involved in the operation. Out of the hijackers, 3 survived and 1 died later from his injuries. Although 4 civilians were wounded, the rest of the remaining crew and all passengers were safely rescued.

The Boeing 737 involved in the hijacking stayed on in service with Lufthansa until 1995 when it was sold to the Brazilian airline TAF Linhas Aéreas and flew with them until 2008.

Operation Storm

Russian military involvement in Afghanistan has a long history, going back to Tsarist expansions in the so-called "Great Game" between Russia and Britain. This began in the 19th century with such events as the Panjdeh Incident, a military skirmish that occurred in 1885 when Russian forces seized Afghan territory south of the Oxus River around an oasis at Panjdeh. This interest in the region continued on through the Soviet era, with billions in economic and military aid sent to Afghanistan between 1955 and 1978.

Operation Storm 333 was the codename of an operation conducted on 27 December 1979 in which Soviet Special Forces stormed the Tajbeg Palace in Afghanistan and killed Afghan President Hafizullah Amin and his 100–150 personal guards. His 11-year-old son died due to shrapnel wounds. The Soviets installed Babrak Karmal as Amins successor. The operation presaged the Soviet invasion of Afghanistan on the same day. Along with President Hafizullah a further 200 personal guards were also killed.

The operation involved 30 men from the 'Grom' (Thunder) unit of the Alpha Group, 30 men of the 'Vympel' Group and 30 men of the 'Zenit' (Zenith) Group. All three of these forces had been raised by the KGB, for counter terrorism, deep penetration and covert operations. The Alpha Group, was more specifically a Special Forces (Spetsnaz) and special operations unit. Attached to the KGB, and had been created on 28 July 1974 within the First Chief Directorate of the KGB on the orders of Yuri Andropov, then chairman of the KGB. It was intended for counterterrorism operations to give the KGB the capacity to respond within the USSR to such incidents as the Palestinian massacre of Israeli athletes at the 1972 Munich Olympics in Germany.

As well as the 90 KGB Special Forces personnel, Operation Storm 333also had 520 men of the 154th Separate Spetsnaz Detachment, made up only of men from the southern republic of the USSR. As well as the 154th, 87 men from the 345th Guards Airborne Regiment. These support troops were not issued with body armour or helmets, whereas the three KGB units had bullet proof body armour and helmets. This was a critical factor as Amin's personal guard totalled around 2,500 men, who were armed only with sub-machine guns, which had low velocity rounds that could not penetrate the Soviet body armour.

The Soviet force approached the target in a convoy of vehicles, many of them in armoured personnel carriers, which were already in Afghanistan as part of the military and technical support for the Afghan government in its fight with major Muslim fundamentalist insurgents in several parts of Afghanistan. By the time of Operation Storm 333, the Soviets had become suspicious of Amin's loyalties and longer-term objectives. This made the Soviet come to the decision that he needed to be replaced by a more compliant communist president. As the vehicles approached their large, they were met with ineffective small arms fire and a shower of grenades. A ZSU-3-4 Shilka, normally used for air defence, let rip with its four 23mm cannons with a devastating effect, killing many of the Afghan guards and reducing the shower of grenades along with setting fire to many of the Afghan Vehicles. The Soviets disembarked from their vehicles and sprinted towards their target. The palace guards continued to fire from the roof with what was now effective fire. The Soviets helmets and body armour protecting the soldiers as they made their way into the target building.

Once inside, each group knew its task and had been fully briefed on the various building internal layouts. Grenades were thrown followed by small arms fire, as each group broke into their assigned rooms and cleared them. As each room was cleared any resistance began to peter out. The Spetznaz finally approached Amin's suite. Amin had been seen earlier, half-dressed shouting to his wife to bring some AK-47s. When the Spetznaz entered the suite, Amin was behind a bar wearing Adidas shorts. As soon as he popped up the first Soviet officer to enter the room and shot him dead.

19 of the Soviet force were killed, along with 50 wounded during Storm 333. Of the 15 dead, two were from Alpha group, three from Zenit group and six from 154th and the rest from the 345th. The Afghan loses were 200 soldiers killed, 200 wounded and 1,700 captured.

The Russian war in Afghanistan began in February 1979, when the Islamic Revolution ousted the American-backed Shah from Afghanistan's neighbour Iran. The United States Ambassador to Afghanistan, Adolph Dubs, was kidnapped by Setami Milli militants and later killed during an assault carried out by the Afghan police, assisted by Soviet advisers. The death of the U.S. Ambassador led to a major degradation in Afghanistan–United States relations.

The United States deployed twenty ships to the Persian Gulf and the Arabian Sea including two aircraft carriers. This led to a constant stream of threats of warfare between the US and Iran. March 1979 marked the signing of the US backed peace agreement between Israel and Egypt. The Soviet leadership saw the agreement as a major advantage for the United States. One Soviet newspaper stated that Egypt and Israel were now "gendarmes of the Pentagon". The Soviets viewed the treaty not only as a peace agreement between their erstwhile allies in Egypt and the U. S. supported Israelis, but also as a military pact. Along with this the U.S. sold more than 5,000 missiles to Saudi Arabia and also supplied the Royalist rebels in the North Yemen Civil War against the Nasserist government. Also, the Soviet Union's previously strong relations with Iraq had recently soured. In June 1978, Iraq began entering into friendlier relations with the Western world and buying French and Italian-made weapons, though the vast majority still came from the Soviet Union, its Warsaw Pact allies, and China. This all set the stage for the Soviet war in Afghanistan, which lasted nine years from December 1979 to February 1989.

It was Part of the wider Cold War, and was fought between Soviet-led Afghan forces against multi-national insurgent groups called the Mujahideen, mostly composed of two alliances – the Peshawar Seven and the Tehran Eight. The Peshawar Seven insurgents received military training in neighbouring Pakistan and China, as well as weapons and billions of dollars from the United States, United Kingdom, Saudi Arabia, and other countries. The Shia groups of the Tehran Eight alliance received support from the Islamic Republic of Iran. Early in the rule of the PDPA government, the Maoist Afghanistan Liberation Organization also played a significant role in opposition, but its major force was defeated by late 1979, prior to the Soviet intervention.

The decade-long war resulted in millions of Afghans fleeing their country, mostly to Pakistan and Iran. Hundreds of thousands of Afghan civilians were killed in addition to the rebels in the war. The initial Soviet deployment of the 40th Army in Afghanistan began on 24 December 1979, under Soviet leader Leonid Brezhnev. The final troop withdrawal started on 15 May 1988, and ended on 15 February 1989, under the last Soviet leader, Mikhail Gorbachev. Due to the interminable nature of the war, the conflict in Afghanistan has sometimes been referred to as the

"Soviet Union's Vietnam War" or the "Bear Trap." Over 14,000 Soviet troops, 18,000 Afghan troops were killed along with an estimated 75,000 to 90,000 Mujahideen. It was a war Russia could not win and became an embarrassment to them. However, it set the stage for the Taliban rule of the country until the War in Afghanistan in 2001, when intervention in the ongoing Afghan civil war by NATO and allied forces. The war followed the terrorist attacks of 11 September 2001, in an effort to dismantle al-Qaeda and eliminate its safe haven in Afghanistan by removing the Taliban from power.

Operation Eagle Claw

The ill-fated Operation Eagle Claw was the very first operation of the newly formed Delta Force. The operation was arranged by the American president at the time, Jimmy Carter, in response to the Iran hostage crisis, and involved rescuing 52 Americans that had been taken captive at the US Embassy in Tehran. The operation was both a military and political failure. Many errors in the planning led to problems in the execution, especially with the aviation side of the operation. The Joint Task Force commander for the operation was Major General James B. Vaught, the fixed-wing and air mission commander was Colonel James H. Kyle, the helicopter commander was Marine Lieutenant Colonel Edward R. Seiffert, and the Delta Force commander were Colonel Charlie Beckwith, a retired US Army Special Forces Officer who was now in charge of the Tehran CIA Special Activities Division paramilitary team. He had been given two assignments; he was to gather information about the hostages, as well as transport the rescue team from Desert Two, the FUP (Forming-Up Point), to the Embassy grounds to stage the actual rescue. The most important intelligence was gathered from the Embassy cook, who had been released by the hostage takers. He revealed that all the hostages were centrally located within the embassy compound, and this would be a key point used in planning the rescue mission.

Three weeks before the operation on 1 April 1980, a US AFCC (Air Force Combat Controller) was flown in to survey the staging area code named Desert One, located in South Khorasan Province of Iran, near Tabas. He was able to fully survey the airstrip and install some remotely controlled infra-red landing lights and a strobe. He also took a soil sample that in the end would prove fruitless. At the time of the survey the desert floor was packed hard, but over the next three weeks an ankle-deep layer of fine sand was deposited on the airstrip by sandstorms.

The whole operation was a complex one and would be staged over two separate nights. The first night would be spent securing Desert One and ensuring 6,000 gallons of aviation fuel that the USAF had brought in was secured. Eight RH-35D Stallion helicopters of the US Marine Corps were due to arrive from the USS Nimitz. These were painted in a desert colour and all markings removed for the operation. The eight helicopters would be used to transport Delta Force from Desert One to Desert

Two. Once at Desert Two, the helicopters, their crews and Delta Force would hide until the next night. On the second night, the actual rescue mission would be mounted. The CIA would bring in trucks to transport Delta Force before driving the trucks containing Delta Force to Tehran. Simultaneously, other US Troops would disable the power in the area close to the embassy. This was intended to slow down any response from the Iranian military's C-130As, with their 20 mm rotary cannons and 40 mm Bofors cannon. The final element was that the army Rangers would capture the nearby Manzariyeh Air Base so that several C-141 Starlifters could arrive for the evacuation of personnel and hostages. Delta Force would assault the Embassy and eliminate the guards. Afterwards, the hostages and Delta Force operatives would rendezvous with the helicopters across the street at the Shahid Shiroudi Stadium. The helicopters would convey everyone back to the C-141s at Manzariyeh Air Base. The operation involved air support via Air Wings 8 operating from USS Nimitz and Air Wings 14 operating from USS Coral Sea.

The rescue team and its equipment, along with fuel, were in MC-130Es, a low-level clandestine penetration aircraft suitable for Special Forces operations. It was a modified C130 with the addition of special electronics and a low radar observant paint. The EC-130H was another modified C130 used for Airborne Communications Jamming. Through the failing light a single C-130E moved fast and low over dark waters toward the coast of Iran. It was a big four-propeller U.S. Air Force workhorse, a C-130, painted in a mottled black-and-green camouflage that made it all but invisible against the black water and the night sky. It flew with no lights. Inside there was an eerie red glow from the plane's blackout lamps, seventy-four men struggled to get comfortable in a cramped, unaccommodating space, with essential supplies packed into the hold as well. The C-130E refuelled in mid-air on the way to Desert One by a KC-135 tanker just off the Iranian coast. The C-130E flew in at 250 feet over the coast of Iran, well below Iranian radar, before it began a gradual climb to 5,000 feet. It was still flying dangerously low, even at that altitude, because the land rose up suddenly, almost in row after row of jagged ridges—the Zagros Mountains, which looked almost jet black in the pilots' night-vision goggles that gave a grey-green tint to everything he viewed. Its terrain-hugging radar was so sensitive that even though the plane was safely above the peaks, the highest ridges triggered a loud, and almost disconcerting sound from the terrain warning system.

The first EC-130E landed at 10:45pm just before, it landed the hidden lights were activated. Other than those lights, the landing was done in a complete blackout. The pilots had night vision goggles in which to see the infra-red landing lights. The first EC-130E call sign, Dragon One, made four passes to ensure there were no obstructions as it was heavily laden and there was a truck trundling along the runway. However, the landing still resulted in substantial wing damage that would require an extensive rebuild, even though the aircraft remained flyable. The soft sand that had covered the hard runway meant the C-130 was enveloped in an almost opaque cloud as it landed and ground to a halt. As soon as it had stopped, the rear ramp was lowered and Rangers roared off in a Jeep and on a motorcycle to give chase to the truck. The tanker truck was smuggling fuel and trying to escape the area. It was soon caught up with and blown up by a LAW fired by one of the Rangers. The Ranger had not realised it was full of fuel. The subsequent explosion lit up the night time sky for miles around and surely alerted the Iranians to the presence of something going on. The explosion and fireball from the tanker aided the landing for the disorientated RH-53D crews that were coming into land, and gave them a strong visual marker. The passenger in the truck was killed instantly, but the driver managed to run away. He was not considered a threat though; due to his involvement in smuggling, it was felt he would not tip off the authorities. Almost at the same time as the tanker had been blown up, an Iranian bus travelled along the runway, which also served as a road. The civilian bus had 43 passengers on board, along with a driver. There was no alternative other than to detain the bus and the passengers until the operation had been completed. The Rangers shot at the bus to disable it, putting a hole in the radiator and bursting a tyre, which presently brought it to a halt. The passengers were offloaded and searched for weapons, before the conclusion was drawn that they were just poor Iranians in the wrong place at the wrong time.

The second and third MC-130Es landed and unloaded their cargo before taking off at 2315 hours to make room for the two EC-130Es to land, along with the 8 RH-53Ds. The assault team that had been brought in consisted of 120 Delta Force operatives along with 12 Rangers and 15 Iranian Americas who would drive the trucks.

The RH-53Ds were given the call sign Bluebeard along with a number between one and eight. One of the RH-53Ds was lost on the way as a warning light came on for a sensor that the pilot interpreted as a cracked rotor blade. The helicopter was left in the desert and its crew picked up by Bluebeard 8. The helicopters continued on before running into unexpected weather in the form of a haboob, a dust storm in which fine sand particles become suspended in the air. Bluebeard 5 suffered erratic flight instrumentation controls after flying into the haboob and had to abort, returning to USS Nimitz as non-visual flying became impossible. Finally, what was left of the now scattered formation of RH-53Ds arrived at Desert One. Bluebeard 2 arrived with a malfunction in its second stage hydraulics system, leaving only the primary system with which to fly the aircraft. Out of the eight helicopters, which were sent to the first staging area, Desert One, only five managed to arrive in an operational condition. With only five, the minimum needed to complete the mission had been met. One of the helicopters on landing, had hit a rut, which had in turn burst a rear tyre causing it to come off the rim of the wheel. The decision to abort was already being discussed by the various commanders who were unable to fully make a decision. There was a refusal to use Bluebeard 2 and a refusal to reduce the size of the Delta Force team. There was the feeling that more helicopters would be lost to failure. One issue with the RH-53D was its notorious ability to fail on cold starts. The EC-130s had used an extra 90 minutes of fuel whilst idling on the ground, although the thought was that since only six helicopters would arrive, there would be more fuel available. 1,000 US gallons could be transferred from the fuel bladders. However, it was found that one of the EC-130s had used all the fuel in its bladder in refuelling just three helicopters, meaning there would be no spare once all six were refuelled. The recommendation to abort was also passed on to the President. Without this extra fuel, the EC-130 needed to leave immediately to ensure it was able to make it to the KC-135 tanker. Bluebeard 3 was currently blocking its path and also needed to be moved so it could be refuelled on the opposite side of the runway.

Bluebeard 3 was unable to move by ground taxi so it was decided the only way to move it was by hover taxi. Using the Combat Controller to direct the helicopter in the dark night conditions. Bluebeard took off and began its hover. The dust its rotors kicked up, forced the Combat Controller to step backwards under the wing of a C-130 so he was better able to see. The pilot in Bluebeard 3 responded by moving forward as well, thinking he was drifting backward and the Combat Controller due to the dust, was his only reference point. In doing so, the RH-53D main rotor struck the EC-130's rear stabilizer. This caused the RH-53D to tip and its blades strike the wing root causing sparks which in turn ignited the now full wing tank. This led to both the RH-53D and EC-130 bursting into flames that quickly engulfed both aircraft as the EC-130 was quickly evacuated. The ammunition started "cooking off," all the various missiles, grenades, explosives, and small arms rounds on both aircraft, causing loud, cracking explosions and throwing out bursts of flame. The Redeye missiles, started to go off, creating smoke trails high into the sky. Finally, the fuel bladders ignited, sending a huge column of flame skyward in a loud explosion that buckled the fuselage of the C-130. All four propellers dropped straight down into the sand still standing upright.

The men inside C-130, had felt the plane begin to shudder, as if the engines were being throttled up ready for takeoff. The hold of the C-130 had no windows, so the men inside couldn't tell if they were moving yet. After the shudder, they heard two dull bangs as if the landing gear had hit a rock or a rut on the runway. One of the men Fitch looked towards the front of the plane only to see flames and sparks. The loadmaster had also seen flames licking their way around the hold and quickly opened the troop door on the port side of the plane. As he opened it, it revealed a wall of flame and the door was quickly shut. They tried the ramp and that too revealed flames, this meant their only way out was via the starboard troop door. The intense heat could already be felt in the hold - men started to leap out even before the door had been fully opened. The speed in which the fire spread was freighting. Men started piling out of it before it was completely open. Flames were spreading fast along the roof, running down the walls on both sides, causing panic amongst the men. Inside the hold was a 1000 Gallon bladder full of aviation fuel that the flames had yet to reach. The initial explosion had blown a crew member from another C-130 some 100 feet away, clean off his feet.

From his position he could see the RH-53D sat on top of the C-130 at a precarious angle engulfed in flames.

The exploding aircraft and ammunition sent flaming bits of hot metal and debris shooting out in all directions across the makeshift airport, riddling the four remaining working helicopters, whose crews jumped out and quickly moved to a safe distance. Most of the men had no idea what was going on; they knew only that a plane and a helicopter had been destroyed. The air over the scene was heavy with the smell of fuel and thick black smoke billowed up skywards. The remaining C-130s began taxiing in different directions away from the intense fire in fear of getting caught up in an even bigger explosion.

Five airmen from the USAF and the three USMC aircrew on the RH-53D all died in the ensuing conflagration. The intense fire reduced some of the bodies to little more than a pile of ash. The pilot and co-pilot, although badly burned, managed to survive the crash. They had jumped from their burning cockpit, hitting the ground quite hard adding to their injuries. It was a tragic loss of life all due to a pilot, following what he thought was the correct command. A shortage of fuel for the EC-130 to make it to its destination also played a part in the decision, on what would be a dangerous manoeuvre in clear conditions. At night with poor visibility made it an almost foolhardy manoeuvre, made worse with pilots that were not specifically trained to fly in such conditions.

There was no choice but to abort the mission; the President had now been made aware of the recommendation. The five RH-53Ds would have to be left behind and would later be put into active service in the Iranian air force, along with the six the Iranians already had. The 130s carried the remaining forces back to Masirah Island, which was being used as an intermediate airfield. Two C-141 medical evacuation aircraft were standing by. They picked up the injured personnel, Delta Force operatives, Rangers, helicopter crews and personnel. The CIA team also went away, unaware that they had been compromised.

America's elite rescue force had lost eight men, seven helicopters, and a C-130, and before it had even made contact with the enemy.

At 1am on the day after the failed attempt, the White House announced the failure of Operation Eagle Claw. The hostage takers, upon realising what had happened, decided to make any further attempt much more difficult by scattering the hostages across Iran. The people on Iranian bus that had been detained were able to give eyewitness accounts of the planned operation to the Iranian security forces.

Even though the first operation had failed, planning began in earnest for a second operation, called 'Project Honey Badger'. Plans and exercise were successfully undertaken, but due to the scattering of hostages, a battalion of soldiers would be required along with approximately 50 aircraft. Helicopters were felt to be too unreliable, so only fixed wing aircraft would be used. One development was the fitting of rockets fore and aft to a C-130 to create the YMC-130H that would allow for STOL (Short Take Off and Landing). The first fully modified aircraft undertook a demonstration flight at Duke Field at Eglin Air Force Base on 29 October 1980. During landing, it's landing brake rockets were fired too soon and caused a hard touchdown, which tore off the starboard wing and started a fire. The change of administration that was on the horizon meant the project was abandoned. Despite the failure of the YMC-130H, the 'Honey Badger' exercise continued until after the 1980 US election when Ronald Reagan became president.

One of the issues with the original operation was the inability of the various forces to work together cohesively, with each one having their own agenda. This led to the creation of a multi-service organisation called USSOCOM (United States Special Operations Command) several years later, which became operational in April 1987. Another issue was the lack of well-trained pilots that could operate at low level and night conditions in support of clandestine and Special Forces missions. This led to the creation of the 160th Special Operations Regiment, also called the Night Stalkers.

President Carter continued to try to secure the hostages' release before his term in office ended. Despite extensive last-negotiations, he did not succeed. Finally, on 20 January 1981, only a matter of minutes after President Carter's term had ended, the 52 US captives still being held in Iran were released, finally ending the 444-day Iran hostage crisis.

Operation Eagle Claw suffered from overly ambitious planning, the wrong hardware, and the absence of a "red team" to point out flaws and vulnerabilities during the planning process. Although out of the failure of Eagle Claw, it helped push military reforms through that had already started under the Carter administration, and gathered speed under Reagan. While no one would ever suspect it based on Eagle Claw, the

U.S. military was in the process of leapfrogging over its competitors in technology, training, and tactics – a sweeping overhaul, still ongoing, which has come to be called the Revolution in Military Affairs. The paradigm shift brought about by digital command, control, and communications, along with "smart" weapons, stealth technology, and other advances, would be showcased in Operation Desert Storm in 1991. These made the commanding of Special Forces much more combined, and an overall battle picture made for easier deployment. More recently drones, such as the Predator have been used to act as an overwatch and scout ahead as Special Forces move in on their target. Even being able to offer limited close air support with two Hellfire missiles being mounted on the MQ-1A and current B model.

Iran did not escape from the hostage crisis unscathed, having gained the lasting enmity of one of the world's great powers. During the Iran-Iraq War of 1980-1988, the U.S. got vengeance by giving technical assistance to Iraqi forces. Which lead to half a million Iranian military casualties, and the U.S. Navy destroyed the Iranian Navy in Operation Praying Mantis in April 1988. On 3 July 1988, the U.S.S. Vincennes accidentally shot down Iran Air Flight 655, killing all 290 people aboard. Khomeini viewed it as deliberate and threw in the towel in the Iran-Iraq War. Shortly Colonel Gadhafi who was believed to behind many of the hostage and terrorist attacks, including the Lockerbie bombing Where a Pan Am Boeing 747, Flight 103 was blown up mid-air over Lockerbie in Scotland in December 1988, killing 270 people, 11 of which were on the ground. Colonel Gadhafi was killed during the Libyan Civil war in 2011.

Operation Nimrod

The sight of the SAS dressed in black coveralls and hoods complete with S6 respirator; and equipped with an MP5 sub machine gun - blowing out the windows of the Iranian Embassy, during the Iranian Embassy siege in 1980. Have become iconic pictures that were splashed across newspapers and TV screens in 1980. These pictures of B Squadron, 22 SAS, was in many ways the starting point of the media frenzy surrounding the SAS and other special forces. The SAS at the time were largely unknown and had just been thrust into the public eye.

Operation Nimrod was the siege of the Iranian Embassy in London. At 1100 hours on 30 April 1980, six Iranian gunmen had forced their way into the embassy overpowering a police officer, PC Trevor Lock and taking 26 hostages. The terrorists called themselves the 'Democratic Revolutionary Front for Arabistan' they demanded the release of 91 political prisoners who were imprisoned in Iran. They also demanded a plane to fly themselves and the hostages out of the UK. The police moved in and cordoned off the area and set up sipper teams whilst negotiations were undertaken.

B Squadron was back at Hereford as it was their turn at being the Anti-Terrorist team. They were immediately put on alert and quickly made their way down to London. As they made their way down to London, Mi5 lowered microphones down the chimney to gather further intelligence. On arrival the SAS studied building plans to formulate a potential attack plan if they were given the nod. Negotiations continued in earnest until at exactly 1345 hours on May 5, three shots were heard via the various listening devices and out on the street. The leader of the terrorists, Awn Ali Mohammed codenamed 'Salim', announced a hostage had been killed and if their demands were not met within 30 minutes the rest of the hostages would be killed. Negotiators tried to stall the terrorists whilst a final decision was made on the next course of action. The terrorists had crossed the line by killing a hostage and use of deadly force by the SAS was authorised. At 1907 hours the police signed over control of the operation to the SAS commanding officer and B Squadron completed final weapons and kit prep ready to launch an assault.

Red and Blue team B Squadron, were already in position, ready to go when the order was given to begin Operation Nimrod, at 1923 hours. Four men from Red Team abseiled down from the roof at the rear of the building, whilst another four men lowered a stun grenade through the skylight on the roof of the building. The stun grenade was due to go off as the windows were blown out with explosive to cause confusion. This timing, however, did not match, after one of the SAS team abseiling down became entangled in his rope. As they tried to untangle him, a window was smashed, which alerted the terrorists to the attack. This led to the command, "Go, Go, Go" being given to the SAS teams. With the SAS staff sergeant still tangled up in his rope, the rest of the team were unable to use explosives on the windows as this would have led to serious injury, so had to smash their way in. The three SAS soldiers entered the building after throwing in stun grenades and in the process starting a fire that started on the curtains that proved to be highly flammable and spread to the surrounding room. The ensuing fire, burst through a window with a very hot flame, this in turn severely burned the entangled SAS sergeant. The team on the roof blew their charges on the skylight, which caused the entire building to shake and sent a plume of smoke high up into the clear blue sky.

Blue Team were slightly behind Red Team as they detonated explosives on a first floor window. Both teams went through the embassy and conducted a sweep using standard room clearing tactics that they had rehearsed hundreds of times back at Hereford. They quickly killed Salim, who was grappling with PC Trevor Lock after he had tackled him, after PC Lock had drawn his pistol, which he had kept hidden since the siege had begun. Moments later two SAS operatives entered the room. They ordered PC Locke to roll clear of Salim and as soon as he was clear Salim was killed by a quick burst of fire from two MP5 sub machine guns. Inside the Telex room on the 2nd floor, the terrorists began firing indiscriminately at their captives, killing one and wounding another. Moments before the SAS burst into the room, the terrorists threw their weapons down and hid themselves amongst their hostages. In what is still thought of as the most controversial incident of the siege - the SAS put the 2 terrorists against the wall and shot them. As they evacuated the hostages, two of the terrorists had secreted themselves amongst the hostages. As the terrorists hid themselves amongst the hostages, one of the terrorists pulled out a Russian grenade. Due to the terrorist being surrounded by hostages a clear shot was not possible. Instead he was pushed down some stairs, where two SAS soldiers quickly shot him dead with a couple of bursts of fire. The whole operation had taken a mere 17 minutes. Five terrorists lay dead along with one dead and two seriously wounded hostages. Fowzi Nejad, the only surviving terrorist, who was later sentenced to life imprisonment for his part in the siege. From that moment forward the thirst for information on the SAS was almost hard to quench, the world and the terrorists knew about the SAS. The terrorists realised that the UK and other countries would use Special Forces to prevent further terrorist acts. The SAS even before the Iranian siege had been involved in the bloody war in Ireland during the 'Troubles' from 1969, undertaking intelligence gathering and trying to track down and disrupt the IRA.

Raid on Pebble Island

The Falklands War began on 2 April 1982, when Argentine forces invaded and occupied the Falkland Islands and South Georgia. The battle was a historical one, focused on ownership of the islands; Argentina felt that they were simply reoccupying land that formerly belonged to them. The battle lasted 74 days and ended with the Argentine surrender on 14 June 1982, when the islands reverted to British control. During the conflict, 649 Argentine military personnel, 255 British military personnel and 3 Falkland Islanders died. The conflict was a difficult one due to the poor weather conditions and the distance that British forces had to travel; the Falkland Islands are over 8000 miles away from the UK, so it took time to get all the necessary forces and equipment in place. The harsh climate also took its toll on men and equipment when they finally made it to the Falklands. The Falklands war was made even more difficult by the harsh environment, it would be conducted in. On 25 May 1982, the British merchant navy ship Atlantic Conveyor was hit by two Exocet missiles, fired by two Argentine Navy Super Étendard jet fighters. The loss of the Atlantic Conveyer also left all the helicopters bar one Chinook destroyed. The rest being destroyed in the subsequent fire caused by the Exocet missiles. The loss of these helicopters would mean British troops would have to march across the Falklands to recapture Stanley. Adding to the difficulties already being faced by British forces.

Ensuring that air attacks could not be contracted from any airstrip was of great importance in order to protect the fleet and troops on the ground. To that end Port Stanley, under the 'Black Buck' operation, was bombed between April and June 1982. The bombs themselves did little damage overall, but the impact on the Argentines meant they may well have moved their aircraft back to Argentina to keep them safe. Several large craters were caused by bombs that took a few days to fill; the Vulcan bombers used in the attacks were in the process of being retired imminently. The airstrip at Pebble Island was too close to the civilian population for a bombing raid, therefore it was bequeathed to the SAS to mount a raid and destroy enemy aircraft, which consisted of the Pucara attack aircraft. The Pucara was a formidable, twin turboprop attack aircraft and posed a real threat to ground forces landing on the Falklands. It bore a mixture of guns, rockets and bombs.

Pebble Island is the fifth largest Island in the Falklands; it is 19 miles long by about four miles wide. It has three high points - First Mountain 909ft, Middle Mountain 702ft and Marble Mountain 778ft - all of which lie in the western portion of the island. The eastern portion of the island has lakes and wetlands, as well as being an area of high conservation value. Its name is believed to have come from the peculiarly spherical pebbles found at its western tip.

On 14 May, two Westland Sea King HC4 helicopters took off from the pitching deck of HMS Hermes into the night's sky to deliver 45 members of the SAS 3.7 miles from an airstrip at Pebble Island. A team from D Squadron had previously done a reconnaissance on Pebble Island by Klepper canoe. The Klepper canoe is a folding canoe, made from a wooden, aluminium and plastic frame with a tough waterproof fabric skin. It is a direct decedent of the Inuit kayak.

As well as the target, D Squadron also noted the weather conditions, such as the strong headwind which would increase flying time and decrease loitering time. This meant the raid would have to be conducted within 30 minutes, instead of the 90 minutes they had hoped for. This changed the target priority to be aircraft first and personnel second. In many ways, this raid was not too dissimilar to the raids performed by David Stirling on airfields in Libya in 1942.

The trip out on the helicopter was a bumpy one, with constant pitching over the rough sea as the Sea Kings flew in at low level. Once at the LZ, the SAS soldiers unloaded all their kit, which comprised of 100 L16 81mm mortar bombs, 66mm Rocket, L1A1 Light anti-tank Weapons and explosive charges to undertake the raid. Each SAS soldier carried at least two mortar bombs and other supplies along with their M16. Some of the M16s were fitted with underslung M203 grenade launchers. The move from their LZ to the airfield was across a very barren and wild, windswept area offering little cover to the SAS men. The cold enveloped them the wind forced its way through any small gap it could find in their clothing. Progress had to be swift as the timings were tight. A cutoff group was put in place to ensure the enemy could not leave or put a counter attack in place. The group also had a mortar team in place to keep the Argentine soldiers pinned down while the attack happened. As the men got close they spotted a lone sentry but were able to get passed him without being seen. The noise of the wind helped drown out whatever noise they made while running. It was not hard to find the aircraft on the airstrip and the SAS began planting charges on them. The charges were placed in the same location on each aircraft to ensure that they could not easily be cannibalised for spare parts. The SAS men set the detonators and re-grouped with the cutoff and fire support teams.

With the charges set, the SAS used rockets and small air fire to further damage the aircraft. Some of the aircraft had their undercarriages completely shot away, but all had varying degrees of impairment. Once the SAS team had regrouped, HE (High Explosive) rounds were fired from HMS Glamorgan. The HE rounds hit the runway, ammunition and fuel dumps, causing much larger explosions. The response from the Argentine soldiers was minimal. The SAS had expected a heavy firefight, but only suffered sporadic and ineffectual fire from the enemy. The Argentines, believing themselves to be under attack, blew charges to destroy the runway, denying its use. In blowing the runway, two SAS Troopers were slightly wounded by flying shrapnel.

The SAS exfiltrated back to the LZ within the remaining 30 minutes and made it back to HMS Hermes by daybreak. There had been plans to return and finish off the defending force, but this was changed at the last minute. Eleven aircraft were destroyed, including six Pucaras, four Turbo Mentor trainer aircraft and one Short SC7 Skyvan transport aircraft. Along with the fuel and ammunition dump, the raid was hailed a complete success and denied the use of six ground attack aircraft on British Forces. Argentine Forces only had 12 Pucaras in total in the Falklands and the SAS had destroyed half the force in one raid.

Achille Lauro Hijacking

On 7 October 1985, four PLF militants seized control of the cruise liner Achille Lauro off the Egyptian coast. The ship was sailing from Alexandria to Port Said. The Achille Lauro was an Italian registered ship. Built between 1939 and 1947 as MS Willem Ruys, a passenger liner for the Rotterdamsche Lloyd. She featured a superstructure very different from other liners of that era; Willem Ruys pioneered low-slung aluminium lifeboats, within the upper-works' flanks. The next ship to adopt this unique arrangement was the SS Canberra in 1961. Today, all cruise ships follow this layout. The ship became the Achille Lauro in 1965 after she was sold to the Flotta Lauro Line. The ship was named after the company owner. It was extensively rebuilt and modernised following an on-board explosion in 1965. The Achille Lauro entered service in 1966 carrying passengers to Sydney, Australia. The ship played a role in evacuating the families of British servicemen caught up in the unrest in Aden, and made one of the last northbound transits through the Suez Canal prior to its closure during the Six Day War. The ship weighed 23,629 tons after refurbishment and was 642ft in length. She stayed in service until 1994 when the ship caught fire and sank in the Indian Ocean off Somalia.

The actual hijacking of the ship ended up taking place sooner than he hijackers had planned. This was due to them being surprised by a crew member who had discovered them. This meant the hijackers had to act immediately. With 400 passengers and the crew as hostage, the heavily armed hijackers ordered the ship set sail for Tartus, in Syria. They also demanded the release of 50 Palestinian prisoners being held in Israeli prisons. Due to the fact that many of the ship's passengers were US citizens, US President Ronal Reagan ordered the deployment of the US Navy SEAL Team six and elements of Delta Force to plan and, if required, execute the recapturing of the ship and rescue all the hostages.

After the Achille Lauro was refused permission to dock at Tartus, the hijackers killed Leon Klinghoffer, a wheelchair bound Jewish-American businessman, shooting him in the forehead and chest. They forced the ship's barber and a waiter to throw his body and wheelchair overboard. Klinghoffer's wife, Marilyn, who had not witnessed the shooting, was told by the hijackers that he had been moved to the infirmary. The Achille Lauro headed back towards Port Said, and after two days of negotiations, the hijackers agreed to abandon the liner in exchange for safe conduct. They were flown towards Tunisia aboard an Egyptian commercial airliner.

President Reagon was furious with what he saw as an Egyptian cave in, to the hijacker's demands. On 10 October 1985, he ordered that the Egyptian airliner should be intercepted by F-14 Tomcat fighters from VF-74 and VF-103 squadrons from the USS Saratoga. The airliner was shepherded across the Mediterranean to land at the US Navy airbase at Signella, a NATO installation near Sicily. Here Bassam al Asker, Ahmad Marrouf al Assadi, Youssef Majed al Molqi and Ibrahim Fatayer Abdelatif were arrested by the Italian authorities. However, the terrorist leader Abu Abbas, was allowed to leave with the other passengers as the airliner was released to complete its flight to Tunis despite protest from the US Government. Egypt also demanded an apology for the forcing of an Egyptian airliner from Tunis to Sicily. The arrest of the four terrorists had only occurred after resolution of a diplomatic dispute between Italy and America. Bettino Craxi, the Italian Prime minister, was adamant that Italy had territorial rights over the NATO base as it lay on Italian national soil. At Sigonella, men of Italy's armed Gendarmerie faced US Special Forces personnel from the Navy SEALs who had flown into Sigonella in two Lockheed C-141 Starlifter's. More of Italy's armed Gendarmerie known as Carabinieri was dispatched from Cataina to reinforce the Italian presence at Sigonella. This was the most difficult crisis in modern Italian and US diplomatic relations, and was resolved in favour of the Italians after a five-hour standoff.

The PLO Foreign Secretary Farouq Qaddumi later denied that the hijackers were responsible for the murder, and suggested that Marilyn had killed her husband for insurance money. Over a decade later, in April 1996, PLF leader Muhammad Zaidan accepted responsibility, and in 1997, the PLO reached a financial settlement with the Klinghoffer family.

Operation Mikado

At the height of the Falklands war, the risk of Exorcet missiles became more and more of a concern. A plan was drawn up, to initially undertake a reconnaissance mission to gather intelligence and look at the feasibility of destroying Exorcet missiles in mainland Argentina, which would be a mission fraught with danger. Operation Mikado utilised B Squadron of the 22nd Special Air Service had been ordered to draw up plans to destroy the Exocets, and the planes that could deliver them on their airbase on the Argentine mainland. Inspired by the Israeli operation at Entebbe, Brigadier Peter de la Billiere, the Director of Special Forces proposed a tactical landing assault on an Argentine air base by the SAS. The plan after the initial reconnaissance mission was to fly Squadron in two C-130 Hercules of RAF Special Forces Flight (47 Sqn) directly from Ascension Island onto the Argentine Rio Grande airbase at Tierra del Fuego. Once on the ground, the 60 or so SAS men would assault the airfield, destroying any aircraft and Exocets present. They would also storm the Officer's mess, taking out the pilots. Following the attack, the SAS would escape and evade to friendly Chile, either on the C-130s, if they survived, or on their own. The Chile boarder was some sixty miles from the airbase.

The preliminary reconnaissance mission, was called 'Operation Plum Duff' which consisted of an eight man team who were to travel to the Argentine Mainland on a stripped out Royal Navy Sea King Mark IV. The Sea King had to be stripped out to lose weight so that it could just make the mainland. The Sea King pilot and two crew would have to ditch the Sea King on their one-way mission. Whichever way you looked at it, Operation Plum Duff was a tall order, made taller by the lack of intelligence, coherent maps or proper briefings. It was clear to every member of the eight-man patrol that they had been asked 'to conduct a full-frontal assault into the unknown.

At 0500 hours on 15 May 1982, 6 Troop would depart; the team would fly to Ascension Island in the South Atlantic. From there they would be taken in a C130 RAF Hercules transport plane to the waters off the Falklands. Following a parachute drop, the Royal Navy would pick them up from the ocean and take them aboard a carrier. Finally, they would get on board a Sea King and fly to Argentina.

The Sea King made it to the Argentine coast undetected, but found itself in fog about 7 miles from the intended drop off point. Fearing the Argentines had spotted them, the decision was made to head for Chile and the SAS would walk the twenty-six miles to the air base. The Sea King crew and the SAS argued over the navigation and position of the Sea King. He Sea King headed or Chillie were the SAS would make it off on foot the few miles to the boarder. As the fog lifted the moon started to shine through, as the Sea King made its final approach the cold night air was further made more inhospitable with pounding sleet and freezing rain. Once on the ground the SASs only option was to start moving eastwards until first light. There was three hours left until first light. Low-lying, gentle hills covered with vast patches of marsh and grass made it hard for the SAS troop to move swiftly. There was snow on the ground and near-freezing rain blew horizontally into their backs. Adding to the discomfort from the bitter cold. The conditions were proving too much for one trooper who had developed a fever and was slowing the troop down. There was no choice but to lay up for twenty-four hours contrary to the orders from Hereford. During the daylight hours of the May 19 and 20, the men lay in their sleet-covered tents called a bivouac conserving energy. In each direction, there was nothing but undulating plains of pampas grass, covered with snow or ice. Reality was closing in. Fast. After dark on the 20 May, the troop resumed their trek that was increasingly becoming pointless. With only two days' rations left, they were still no closer than ten miles from the border of Argentina, and from there the target was a further 20 miles across enemy territory. The SAS troop was in need of a re-supply if they were to be able to continue on to their objective. When asked, Hereford decided that the SAS troop was to head back to an ERV (Emergency Rendezvous) point that would be manned by an SAS Officer Captain Pete Hogg. Hogg had originally flown into Chile to debrief the Royal Marines that had been captured in South Georgia on April 1982 and released.

The Royal Marines are worth noting for their outstanding performance during the Falklands war in several key battles. The one in which Hogg was debriefing was for those that had fought in a in a modern day "Rorke's Drift" on South Georgia, when 22 Marines had held off Argentine forces. Downing two Puma helicopters as well as an undisclosed number of Argentine soldiers. The Argentines had no idea they had fought against just 22 Royal Marines after a 'brilliant bit of British bluff', when Lieutenant Mills walked brazenly towards the Argentinians and warned his men would keep fighting unless they agreed to his terms - including safe passage off the island, the Argentinians agreed. Captain Lawrence, leading the SAS troop had never been made aware that such an emergency plan would or could be activated. A meeting place was to be a bridge chosen via a map that had no grid or contours. Hogg was due to meet the SAS troop the following night. The ERV would be open for just one hour after sunset. After the communication arranging the ERV, the SAS troop's radio died and were unable to contact anyone. By late afternoon on 22 May 1982, 6 Troop believed they were in the correct location. They went to ground and waited until dusk – nothing happened, nor for the next three days.

On the morning of 26 May, Lawrence and another trooper slipped their civilian camping coats over their camouflaged jackets, and put 9mm Browning pistols in their pockets before heading off to the nearest town, Porvenir, more than 50 miles away.

They hitched on a logging truck hoping at some point to be able to make a telephone call to the British consul. In Porvenir, they were directed towards a wooden hut, where a single communal radio telephone was operated by a single man.

The consul came on the line. But the counsel was terrified as he had not been briefed. The counsel, recommended that the SAS troop give themselves up. Which was quite an unexpected reply. Lawrence was walking around Porvenir the same evening when he bumped into the SBS that had been sent in to rescue the SAS troop.

For reasons that are still unknown to this day, the troop sent to rescue the SAS troop had made no attempt to make their way to the ERV. Finally, on 30 May the SAS troop was boarded onto a plane bound for Santiago in great secrecy, before being ordered home on 8 June.

Shortly after landing in Chile the crew of the Sea King tried to unsuccessfully sink the Sea King. So, instead they decided to set it alight, before making good their escape. Setting the Sea King alight required a cover up story from the MOD when it was found a few days later, stating it was on anti-submarine patrol and ran into mechanical difficulty ditching their helicopter.

Whilst Plum Duff was underway, B Squadron began practicing for the assault operation, code named 'Operation Mikado'. Dry runs against British airfields began to highlight problems with the plan. The large C-130s would appear on radar screens, giving the defenders ample time to prepare to repel the attack. Even at very low level the C-130s had been just too large to be able to hide from radar even if they flew at treetop height. If an attempt had been made to land with the C-130s clearly lighting up the radar screens and having to slow down to land – anti aircraft fire would have cut the plane to shreds and the Argentines would have also blocked the runway. Without the element of surprise, the SAS stood little chance of undertaking a successful raid even if they did manage to land and get off the C-130s. Further issues were around the available intelligence and the precise location of the Super Etendard Jets from the French company Dassault-Breguet along with the Exorcet missiles. The planes and missiles may not be there when the SAS arrived. Even if they were all there, the SAS had no idea where the Exorcet missiles were located on the air base. With all these issues there was no real choice but to scrub Operation Mikado in its current form. The threat from Exorcet missiles was still an issue that needed to be dealt with, so the SAS devised plan B.

This time the plan would be to insert themselves into Argentina via Gemini inflatables launched from the deck of a Royal Navy Submarine, just off the coast of Argentina. The SAS would in a true World War Two, David Stirling type raid, sneak into the airbase and plant explosives on the planes, before escaping on foot into Chile. Before the raid could be put into action, the Argentines surrendered at Port Stanley and the Falklands War was over. If the SAS had attempted an attack on Rio Grande hey would have been met by 3 battalions of Argentine Marines. Stacking the odds of success as almost impossible.

Operation Urgent Fury

On 19 October, 1983, Grenadian Prime Minister Maurice Bishop and a number of his top aides were executed by the PRA (People's Revolutionary Army) on orders from the 'Revolutionary Military Council,' a radical new political group. They were intending to replace Bishop's Marxist government with an even more virulent Marxist regime. General Hudson Austin and his 16-member RMC quickly moved to gain control of the island nation. The US was fearful of a new Soviet ally that was a bit too close for comfort to its own shores. Their fear was bolstered by the recent construction of a 10,000-foot runway, which would enable the largest military transports to land there. This, and the fact that hundreds of US citizens resided in Grenada and may be in imminent danger, prompted President Reagan to act in order to prevent a potentially grave situation from developing. He authorised the US military to intervene and carry out an evacuation operation to rescue American students and, in no small part, to restore a more mainstream government in Grenada.

The mission was named Operation Urgent Fury. It would involve special operations forces from all service branches. Included in the battle plan were US Navy SEALs and Special Boat Units, Marine reconnaissance and Force Recon, Air Force special tactics teams (PJ and CCT) and AC-130 gunships, Army Rangers and Delta Force, and PSYOPS and Civil Affairs units. These groups made up a large part of the total initial force to be deployed in the early stages of the invasion. Also included were elements of two recently formed and highly secret counter terrorist units: SEAL Team Six, now famous for the capture of Osama bin Laden in 2011, and Delta Force.

The two primary objectives for Delta Force's assault were Fort Rupert and Richmond Hill prison. Fort Rupert was reported to be housing the core of senior advisers to General Austin, collectively known as the Revolutionary Council. Richmond Hill prison was holding scores of illegally imprisoned civil servants, along with other citizens arrested by the oppressive RMC regime. Ideally, Delta Force would have preferred conduct these operations at night, under the cover of darkness. Night conditions were also favoured by the pilots and crew that would undertake the mission. The newly formed 160th Special Operations Group, known also as Task Force 160 but better known as the 'Night

Stalkers,' also preferred night ops. 160th Special Operations Aviation Regiment consists of the best aviators and was borne out of the failed Eagle Claw Operation and the need for specially trained aviation crews to support and transport troops in hostile environments. The pilots are trained to fly at very low levels and conduct most of their missions at night, hence the name 'Night Stalkers'. There is a current total of 184 helicopters that consist of 51 MH/AH-6M Little Birds, 61 MH-47G Chinooks and 72 MH-60M Black Hawks (including several top-secret Black Hawks used in Operation Neptune Spear in 2011). In Grenada the 160th would be used to transport and exhilarate SF from their various hostile targets. As soon as it was known of pending actions in Grenada, the 160th dispatched a number of Black Hawks from Fort Campbell, Kentucky to a nearby island staging area in Barbados. The 'Little Birds' were simultaneously transported by Air Force C-5 and C-130 cargo planes to a secret location to meet up with Delta Force operators who had arrived from Fort Bragg and prepare for the mission.

Richmond Hill prison was built on the site of an old fort overlooking the town of St. George's. The prison was in turn overlooked by Fort Frederick, which was manned by a heavily-armed garrison of the People's Revolutionary Army. Between the prison and the fort was a small valley, and it was through this valley that the assault team would have to fly. Upon arrival at the prison, the helicopters would move to their designated location around the facility and get into a hover before the Delta Force operators fast-roped to the ground and began their assault.

The original plan called for nine helicopters, taking both Delta Force operators and elements of Charlie Company, 1/75th Rangers. They were due to leave at 1am, but due to chaotic planning, last minute arguments and rivalry between services at senior levels, it was 6:30am before they departed, five and a half hours behind schedule. This changed it from a night raid to a daylight raid, increasing the risks and making it a far more dangerous mission, especially on insertion. Enemy forces would already be aware of the invasion that had begun some hours earlier and would be able to spot and get ready for the approaching helicopter assault force sooner. Intelligence said the prison was lightly defended, but this intelligence would prove wrong. The nine Black Hawks raced toward the prison. As they got close, they saw that there were two enemy gun positions with ZSU-23-2 anti-aircraft guns which had not been picked up by intelligence. The gun positions were visible on a ridge about 150 feet above the prison. It was a perfect commanding location to engage any forces trying to land nearby. The dark colouring of the Black Hawks made them stand out against the early morning sky; as they raced in, they were engaged by anti-aircraft fire and one Black Hawk was shot down. Close air support aircraft were engaged elsewhere and unable to take out the positions. Due to the heavy volume of AAA being directed at them, it quickly became clear that this was going to be almost impossible without putting all involved in extreme, and unacceptable, risk. The Black Hawks tried via the gunner crews they had aboard, to give suppressing fire, but to no avail. There was no choice but to abort and reattempt the raid, which turned out to be equally unsuccessful.

The raid at Fort Rupert was successful, however. Arriving by helicopter, Delta troopers assaulted the complex and rounded up their targets quickly without suffering any casualties. Black Hawks from the 160th picked them up and transported them back to USS Guam without incident. What the failed raid had proven at Richard Hill was that no matter how well trained and skilful forces are, they cannot overcome poor or inaccurate intelligence. If the gun positions had been known, close air support would have been despatched to deal with them prior to the Black Hawks' arrival in the area. The inter-service bickering and last minute changes that led the mission to switch from a night time op to a daytime one made it even more deadly. The British Army has a saying: "Piss poor planning leads to piss poor performance." This was certainly a factor in the Richard Hill raid. And while some missions may succeed on the sheer will and determination of the personnel on the ground, the responsibility for failures such as those experienced at Richmond Hill. Does not lie in the hands of the SF carrying out the actual raid, but with those who send them into harm's way without the best intelligence, support and mission focus possible.

Operation Argon

Operation Argon was an operation carried out by the South African Special Forces 'Recces' during the South African Border War. The operation was to carry out the destruction of the oil facilities at Cabinda Gulf, along with, disrupting the foreign exchange received by Angola from the sale of the oil. South Africa established a Special Forces capability in 1968, in line with international military trends. Initial planning and formation occur, including visits to and studies of foreign Special Forces along with formulation of appropriate structures and techniques for an African context, and formation and training of a core group of founder members. The Recce special forces team was set up in 1972 with the establishment of 1 Reconnaissance Commando at the Infantry School at Oudtshoorn, South Africa. 1 Reconnaissance Commando was founded by General Fritz Loots - the founder of the South African Special Forces, and the first General Officer Commanding of the South African Special Forces. He appointed 12 qualified paratroopers known as "The Dirty Dozen" as the founder members. Included in these 12 paratroopers was Jan Breytenbach, who was placed in command of the Founder Members by General Loots.

The South African Border War, took place from 1966 to 1989 largely in South-West Africa and Angola between South Africa and its allied forces, mainly the National Union for the Total Independence of Angola, UNITA on one side and the Angolan government, South-West Africa People's Organisation (SWAPO), and their allies on the other. It was closely intertwined with the Angolan Civil War and the Namibian War of Independence. Namibian gained its independence in 1990.

On 13 May 1985, a South African Navy strike craft carrying a Recce team as well as a back-up team left Saldanha Bay, 65 miles northwest of Cape Town in South Africa and travelled to a spot some way off the Angolan coast near its border with Zaire. The mission was to confirm the existence of ANC (African National Congress) bases and South-West Africa People's Organisation (SWAPO) bases near Cabinda. The area contained oil storage installations run by the Angolans and Gulf Oil. Due to the large oil storage, several large military bases were also in the vicinity. Speculative reports had mentioned U.S. veterans and ex-SAS guarding the installations.

The Recces landed on the coast at night on 20 May 1985, following an advance scouting party sent to gather intelligence on the beach where the party would land. Under ideal cloudy skies, the Recce team's trip had been slowed by the need to launch their boats further from shore than anticipated. This meant a longer journey, coupled with rough seas, threw off the precise timing of the mission. Near the shore, Captain Wynand Du Toit noticed a small fishing vessel in the area of the landing zone and that the occupants were on shore around a fire. Not wanting to be detected meant the team had to wait offshore, until the boat left the area. They were now three hours behind schedule, and the danger of being detected grew.

Upon landing the boats were hidden and RV set up. The men climbed a bluff and followed a route that skirted a small village that led to a road. They miscalculated the distance to the road and turned back, losing an hour of valuable time. Du Toit decided to continue and reach the LUP (Lying Up Position) in a densely wooded area two hours prior to dawn. South African Intelligence and aerial photographs showed an uninhabited area, but in fact it was surrounded by camouflaged People's Armed Forces for the Liberation of Angola (FAPLA) bases. The hide was finally reached as day broke. This proved to be far from ideal as a hiding place, as it was not part of the jungle, but an island of dense growth some distance from the jungle. The Recces hid in the undergrowth and spread into a defensive perimeter, one man at an observation post several yards to the north with a view of the course they had travelled.

As dawn broke, the features of a well-hidden FAPLA base became clear some 1,000 yards (910 m) from the LUP. A few hours later, a small FAPLA patrol could be seen following the tracks they had left the night before. The team watched as the patrol withdrew, and came back with a much larger patrol which passed the hide. At 1700 a three man patrol followed the team's trail directly to the thicket where the Recce's were hidden. They stopped short of entering the brush, and returned to their base. Meanwhile a second patrol approached the hide from the other direction, and opened up with heavy fire on the Recce position. As RPGs struck their position, Captain Du Toit ordered the withdrawal of his troops. They had no choice but to double back on the trail that brought them to this position the previous night. Two of the men were wounded as they exited the trees. FAPLA troops deployed 46 m west of the site opened up with RPD machine guns a 7.62mm light machine gun developed in the Soviet Union in 1945 by Vasily Degtyaryov for the intermediate 7.62x39mm M43 cartridge. RPGs and many AK-47s rained down on the Recce team. The team turned north, pursued by FAPLA soldiers. Another group of Angolan soldiers advanced from the west, flanking the Recce's so that they could only go east now. They could see a group of trees, but needed to cross 37 m of waist-high grass to get to the cover.

Du Toit took two men and made his way through the grass as the rest of the team hid in the thicket. The small team drew fire as over 30 troops moved onto the exposed position. Bullets were cracking through the air as the Recce's tried their best to hold off the attackers. The attackers being numerically superior and having a firepower advantage continued to advance. One Recce, Corporal Rowland Liebenberg, was killed as his two comrades fought on. The fighting continued for a full 45 minutes before two men started to run out of ammunition and were both wounded, Sergeant Louis van Breda later died and Du Toit only just pulled through.

When the firefight was over and two South African soldiers were dead. While Du Toit lay on his stomach, FAPLA soldiers approached and, thinking he was also dead, stripped his equipment – only then, did they realise he was alive and shot him again through the neck. He remained awake with wounds in his neck, shoulder and arm as the FAPLA soldiers began to savagely beat him. The soldiers thought that he was a mercenary, though Du Toit tried to explain that he was in fact a South African Army officer. After being severely roughed up, he was finally taken to Cabinda for medical treatment to a Luanda hospital. The remaining six Recce soldiers carefully made their way north, where they regrouped and were eventually picked up to be returned safely to South Africa. Their escape was mainly due to being ignored after the Angolans captured Du Toit. Allowing them to quietly slip away undetected. Du Toit was finally to be released on 7 September 1987 after 837 days in solitary confinement in an Angolan prison. His release was due to a complicated prisoner exchange arrangement. The exchange took place in Maputo, Mozambique were Du Toit was swapped for two ANC members and 133 Angolan soldiers.

Egypt Air Flight 648

A Boeing 737-200 airliner, EgyptAir Flight 648 was, hijacked on 23 November 1985 by the terrorist organization Abu Nidal. The subsequent raid on the aircraft by Egyptian troops resulted in dozens of deaths, making the hijacking of Flight 648 one of the deadliest such incidents in history. Unit 777 involved in the ill-fated rescue mission, also known as Task Force 777, is an Egyptian military counterterrorism and special operations unit created in 1978 by the government of Anwar Sadat in response to concerns of increased terrorist activity following the expulsion of Soviet military advisors from the country by Sadat and his efforts to achieve peace with Israel. In 1978, Egyptian Army Special Forces were dispatched to Larnaca International Airport, Larnaca, Cyprus in response to the hijacking of a Cyprus Air passenger aircraft by operatives of the PFLP. The operation was organized hastily, and Egyptian authorities failed to notify Cyprus of the arrival of the unit covered earlier on in this book. The aftermath of the failed incident and the need of a professional counterterrorism unit in Egypt resulted in the creation of Unit 777.

On 23 November 1985, Flight 648 took off at 2000 hours on its Athens, Greece to Cairo, Egypt route. Ten minutes after takeoff, three Palestinian members of Abu Nidal hijacked the aircraft. The terrorists, calling themselves the Egypt Revolution, were heavily armed with guns and grenades. The terrorist leader, Omar Rezaq, proceeded to check all passports of the passengers on board the plane. At this point, an Egyptian Security Service agent, Mustafa Kamal, aboard decided to open fire, killing one terrorist before being wounded himself along with two flight attendants. In the exchange of fire, the fuselage was punctured, causing a rapid depressurisation. This meant the plane needed to descend quickly to a safe height of 14,000 feet so that the passengers, crew and hijackers did not suffer from hypoxia.

Libya was the original intended destination for the hijackers, but due to the negative publicity the hijacking would have had, if it was flown to Libya, coupled with the fact that the plane did not have enough fuel, Malta was chosen as a more suitable option. The aircraft was running dangerously low on fuel, experiencing serious pressurisation problems and carrying a number of wounded passengers. However, Maltese authorities did not give permission for the aircraft to land. The Maltese government had previously refused permission to other hijacked aircraft. EgyptAir 648 hijackers insisted, and forced the pilot, Hani Galal, to land at Luqa Airport. As a last-ditch attempt to stop the landing, the runway lights were switched off, but the pilot managed to land the damaged aircraft safely, without further damage to the aircraft.

At first, Maltese authorities were optimistic they could solve the crisis. Malta had good relations with the Arab world, and 12 years earlier had successfully resolved a potentially more serious situation when a KLM Boeing 747 landed there under similar circumstances. However, the Maltese were still very inexperienced in dealing with terrorists and hijackers. The authorities took a firm stand in denying fuel to the hijackers, but made no sensible provisions, through political bias and lack of experience, to meet the circumstances that arose from this decision. No proper team was set up at the outset to evaluate or deal progressively with the crisis, although only a few days previously an incident management course had been organized by a team of U.S. experts in Malta at the request of the government. The Maltese Prime Minister, Dr. Karmenu Mifsud Bonnici, rushed to the airport's control tower and assumed responsibility for the negotiations. Aided by an interpreter, he refused to refuel the aircraft, or to withdraw Maltese armed forces that now surrounded the plane, until all passengers were released. Eleven passengers and two injured flight attendants were allowed off the plane. The hijackers started shooting hostages, starting with Tamar Artzi, an Israeli woman. She was grazed on the ear, but pretended to be dead. Rezaq, the chief hijacker, threatened to kill a passenger every 15 minutes until his demands were met. His next victim was Nitzan Mendelson, another Israeli woman. She was killed instantly. He shot three Americans - Patrick Scott Baker, Scarlett Marie Rogenkamp and Jackie Nink Pflug. Of the five passengers shot, Artzi, Pflug and Baker survived.

France, Great Britain and the United States all offered to send Special Forces to aid in a rescue attempt. Bonnici was under heavy pressure from both the hijackers and the United States and Egypt, whose ambassadors were at the airport. The non-aligned Maltese government feared that the Americans or the Israelis would arrive and take control of the area, as the U.S. Naval Air Station Sigonella was only 20 minutes away.

A U.S. Air Force C-130 Hercules with an aeromedical evacuation team from Rhein-Main Air Base (2nd Aeromedical Evacuation Squadron) near Frankfurt, Germany, and rapid-deploying surgical teams from Wiesbaden Air Force Medical Center were on standby at the U.S. Navy Hospital in Naples. When the U.S. told Maltese authorities that Egypt had a Special Forces counterterrorism team trained by the U.S. Delta Force ready to move in, they were granted permission to come. The Egyptian Al-Sa'iqa, Task Force 777, under the command of Major-General Kamal Attia were flown in. They were led four American officers. Negotiations were stretched out as much as possible, and it was agreed that the plane should be attacked on the morning of November 25 when food was to be taken into the aircraft. Soldiers dressed up as caterers would jam the door open and attack.

Without warning, around an hour and a half before the planned time of the raid, Egyptian commandos attacked the passenger doors and luggage compartment doors with explosives. Bonnici claimed that these unauthorized explosions caused the internal plastic of the plane to catch fire, causing widespread suffocation. The other theory is that when the hijackers realised that they were being attacked, they lobbed hand grenades into the passenger area, killing people and starting an on board fire. However, both the Egyptian explosives and the hijackers' grenades could have been responsible for the fire and deaths. As passengers tried to escape the burning plane they were shot and killed by snipers, who believed they were the hijackers.

The storming of the aircraft killed 54 of the remaining 87 passengers, as well as two crew members and one hijacker. Only one hijacker, Omar Rezaq, who had survived, managed to remain undetected by the Maltese government. The terrorist leader, who was injured during the storming of the aircraft, had removed his hood and ammunition and pretended to be an injured passenger. Egyptian commandos tracked Rezaq to St. Luke's General Hospital and, holding the doctors and medical staff at gunpoint, entered the casualty ward looking for him. He was arrested when some of the passengers in the hospital recognized him.

A total of 58 of the 95 passengers and crew had died, as well as two of the three hijackers, by the time the crisis was over. Maltese medical examiners estimated that four passengers had been killed by bullets fired by Task Force 777.

Rezaq faced trial in Malta, but with no anti-terror legislation, he was tried on other charges. There was widespread fear that terrorists would hijack a Maltese plane or carry out a terror attack in Malta as an act of retribution. Rezaq received a 25-year sentence, of which he served eight. His release caused a diplomatic incident between Malta and the U.S. because Maltese law strictly prohibited trying a person twice, in any jurisdiction, on charges connected to the same series of events. Following his immediate expulsion on release, he was captured on arrival in Nigeria. After three months he was handed over to the U.S., brought before a U.S. court and, on 7 October 1996, sentenced to life imprisonment with a no-parole recommendation.

Task Force 777 had badly handled the rescue mission leading to a massacre. Task Force 777 had been given too much freedom and they undertook their mission with little regard for the safety of the passengers. They were more focused on killing or capturing the hijackers than rescuing the passengers and crew. They were determined to get the hijackers at all costs and the Maltese government's initial refusal for U.S. anti-terrorist resources, which was a team led by a major-general with listening devices and other equipment to aid in intelligence gathering and threat assessment, offered by the State Department through the U.S. Embassy in Malta. It was a decision that was reversed too late and contributed in no small measure to the mismanagement of the entire operation. The fire could well have been made worse by the Task Force 777s positioning of explosives in the hold very close to oxygen tanks which blew up.

Much was to be learned from the operation and also got Task Force 777 off to a bad start on the worlds Special Forces stage.

Ambush at Loughall

The 'Troubles' in Northern Ireland were long and bloody. They began in the late 1960s and continued until the "Good Friday" Agreement in 1998. However, since then there has still been sporadic violence. The key issues at stake during the Troubles were the constitutional status of Northern Ireland and the relationship between its mainly Protestant Unionist community and its mainly Catholic nationalist community. Irish nationalists and republicans generally want Northern Ireland to leave the United Kingdom and join a united Ireland, while unionists and loyalists wanted Northern Ireland to remain within the United Kingdom. The Troubles involved republican and loyalist paramilitaries, the security forces of the United Kingdom and of the Republic of Ireland, and politicians and political activists.

In May 1987 British Intelligence got word of a planned IRA attack on a police station in Loughgall, County Armagh. The SAS was tasked with preparing an ambush to intercept the attackers. The intelligence that had been gained had most likely come from an IRA mole planning the attack. In 1986 a JCB digger had been used to blow up a police station and the attack in Loughall was to follow a similar plan. The JCB's front bucket would be packed with explosives and driven at the police station before exploding.

The RUC's (Royal Ulster Constabulary) E4A covert intelligence unit had located the stolen JCB and suspected the East Tyrone Active Service Unit was the ones planning the attack. Reports of a Toyota Hiace van being stolen by masked men also began to surface.

At just after 1900 hours on 8 May 1987, Declan Arthurs, a member of the IRA, drove a stolen JCB 3CX excavator with a bomb in its bucket through the perimeter fence of the police station. The bomb in the bucket was made up of 200lb of Semtex that had been placed within an oil drum. Finally, it had been wired to explode via two 40 second fuses. The farmer who owned the JCB had been held hostage at gunpoint since it had been stolen to ensure that he did not alert the authorities. The previously stolen blue Toyota Hiace van pulled up and screeched to a stop before the doors flung open and the IRA members jumped out, opening fire on the police station. While this was happening, Tony Gormley lit the bomb fuses with a Zippo lighter. Within moments of the IRA attack commencing, the SAS sprung their ambush and opened fire with M16 and H&K G3 rifles and L7A2 general purpose machine guns. The H&K G3 rifles were particularly effective as they had a 7.62 round, compared to the 5.56 rounds in the M16, giving them greater stopping power. They were unable to stop the bomb detonation, even though the SAS had sprung the ambush from both sides of the road adjacent to the police station. In the process of detonation, the JCB was destroyed and the building blown in half, leaving half standing and half a pile of rubble. In the explosion, three members of the security forces were wounded.

The SAS continued to lay down fire, riddling both the JCB and the Toyota with bullets. In total, they fired approximately 600 rounds between them. The IRA managed to return about 70 rounds in the ensuing but short-lived firefight, but the fire they returned was totally ineffective. The IRA team were out in the open with no cover except for the van through which bullets were passing. Within a matter of minutes, all eight IRA members had been shot and killed, most having been shot through the head as they were wearing bullet-proof vests. However, these did not have any ballistic plates in them so we're unable to stop the larger calibre rounds of the machine guns and rifles the SAS were using. As they were engaged in the fire fight, a car containing Antony Andrews and his brother Oliver came upon the scene. They were returning home from work and on seeing what was happening, Antony put the car into reverse, to get away as quickly as possible. The SAS attention was diverted to the noise and they assumed it was more IRA fleeing. The SAS opened fire and shot around 40 rounds at the fleeing car. Antony Hughes died at the scene, while Oliver was rushed to the Royal Victoria hospital and made a full recovery. They were both dressed in civilian clothes and there was no real reason to suspect they were IRA. They were quite simply in the wrong place at the wrong time and during the ambush, split decisions had to be made with tragic consequences. Antony Hughes' widow was later compensated by the British government for the death of her husband.

In the aftermath, the security forces recovered a firearm from each of the now dead IRA members at the scene, along with three H&K G3 rifles, one FN FAL rifle, two FN FNC rifles, a Ruger Security Six revolver and a Franchi SPAS-12 shotgun. The RUC were later able to link the guns to seven murders and twelve attempted murders in the Mid Ulster area. The Ruger had actually been stolen from a Reserve RUC officer, William Clement, killed two years earlier in the attack on Ballygawley RUC barracks by the same IRA members. Reserve RUC officers are volunteer police officers, much like special constables in the UK. It was also found that one of the other firearms recovered had been used in the killing of Harold Henry, a key contractor to the British Army and RUC in Northern Ireland. The six IRA men killed were IRA 'Commander' Patrick Kelly, 32; Declan Arthurs, 21; Seamus Donnelly, 19; Michael Gormley, 25; Eugene Kelly, 25; James Lynagh, 31, Patrick McKearney, 32 and Gerard O'Callaghan, 29.

The East Tyrone Brigade continued to be active in Ireland until the last IRA ceasefire ten years later. They tried to find out who the informer was but never succeeded. One belief was that the informer was killed during the ambush by the SAS. The IRA men involved in the attack became known as the "Loughgall Martyrs" among the republicans. The relatives of the men considered their killings to be part of a deliberate shoot-to-kill policy by the security forces.

Thousands of people attended their funerals; the largest number of republican funerals in Northern Ireland since those of the IRA hunger strikers of 1981. It was also the single largest loss of IRA life during the Troubles. Gerry Adams, during his graveside oration, gave a speech saying that the British government understood it could buy off the government of the Republic of Ireland, which he described as the "Shoneen Clan" (pro-British), but he added, "It does not understand the Jim Lynaghs, the Pádraig McKearneys or the Séamus McElwaines. It thinks it can defeat them. It never will."

Loughgall RUC station was rebuilt and transferred to the PSNI in 2001, before finally being closed in August 2009 and eventually being sold for private development in April 2011.

Operation Flavius

By 1988, the IRA were still reeling from the Ambush at Loughgall and wanted further retribution in every sense. Later, in March 1988, after Operation Flavius, Corporals David Howes and Derek Wood, two British Army soldiers of the Royal Corps of Signals, were killed by the IRA. On 19 March 1988, the out-of-uniform soldiers were shot after accidentally driving into the funeral procession of an IRA volunteer in Belfast. Three days earlier, loyalist volunteer Michael Stone had attacked an IRA funeral and killed three people. The IRA believed it to be another loyalist attack, and dozens of mourners attacked the soldiers' car. During the attack, Corporal Wood drew his service pistol and fired a shot in the air. This angered the IRA further as they believed they would be shot. The soldiers were dragged from their vehicle and beaten, before being driven to the nearby waste ground, stripped and shot dead

In early March 1988, British Intelligence became aware of a potential IRA plot to attack a parade of British military bands in Gibraltar. This posed a real threat and was passed to the SAS to try and intercept the IRA cell. The mission was given the name 'Operation Flavius.' The British intelligence service believed that the IRA planned to set the bomb off in Gibraltar. The Spanish security services had been watching a three-person cell in Spain. The cell was made up of two men, Danny McCann and Seán Savage, and a woman named Mairéad Farrell. The belief was that they planned to cross into Gibraltar and place explosives in the boot of a car, before placing the car at the assembly point for the parade, which was next to Inces Hall. The Royal Anglian Regiment, which had been present on Bloody Sunday in Derry, Northern Ireland, would be present. Bloody Sunday was the name given to the day when 26 unarmed civil rights protesters and bystanders were shot by soldiers of the British Army on 30 January 1972. To ensure they had the best spot available to detonate the bomb, they parked another car that would appear unconnected, until they were ready to replace it with the car which was rigged with explosives.

On 5 March 1988, Savage was spotted parking a white Renault 5 car. The thought was that it might be the car carrying explosives. Following this sighting, McCann and Farrell had just crossed the border from Spain into Gibraltar. All three of them were under 24-hour observation by intelligence operatives. Savage was seen linking up with McCann and Farrell at around 2:50pm and seemed to be talking while looking intently at the white Renault. They left the area and returned later, appearing to continue paying close attention to the white Renault. The IRA team split up again; Savage headed back into the town and McCann and Farrell headed back to the Spanish border.

When all three of them were well clear of the parked car, an army explosives expert did a walk-by to look for any tell-tale signs of a car bomb, such as exposed wires or the car sitting low due to the weight of explosives in the boot. He did not flag anything up as suspicious, although the car could have been filled with lightweight plastic explosives. However, a concern was raised with the aerial for the radio on the car. The commanders of the operation believed there was a very high likelihood that the Renault contained a bomb.

As per normal operating procedures, the local police chief signed over control of the operation to the SAS, who were to move in and attempt to arrest the IRA unit after the identities of the three suspected IRA members had been positively confirmed. The SAS troopers were dressed in civilian clothing. They were equipped with covert radios and carried 9mm Browning High Power pistols concealed beneath their clothing. The SAS team split into groups so they could follow Savage, McCann and Farrell. They were just about to move in when a local police officer, who was running late and stuck in traffic, put his lights and sirens on. The sirens caused McCann and Farrell to react and on glancing round, McCann seemed to make eye contact with one of the SAS soldiers who were shadowing them. In the debriefing notes, it says that the soldier concerned saw McCann go for something in the front of his jacket. The SAS soldier instantly thought he was either withdrawing a weapon, or triggering the bomb, so he opened fire and took McCann out instantly. Farrell also looked like she was going for something in her bag and was shot several times, along with McCann, by another SAS soldier.

Even though Savage was further down the road, he became alerted to the sound of gunfire and as he turned round, was challenged by two SAS soldiers. Again, according to the debrief notes, Savage ignored the challenge and also moved his hand towards the inside of his jacket. The two SAS soldiers instantly opened up on him with their pistols. As the police approached the scene, the SAS soldiers put on their berets and armbands to identify who they were. On the surface, it looked like a very successful operation that had foiled a major bomb threat. However, it turned out that the three suspected IRA terrorists were unarmed and had no trigger devices on them. Furthermore, upon inspection, the Renault was found to contain no explosives. It was a propaganda coup for the IRA, who turned it into an execution. A bomb that was linked back to the IRA trio in Gibraltar was eventually found in Spain. The thought was that the Renault that Savage had parked was the car being used to reserve the spot in which the car carrying the bomb would later be parked.

The IRA retaliated for the killing by attempting to assassinate Air Chief Marshal Sir Peter Terry at his home in Staffordshire in revenge for his role in Operation Flavius. Terry, at the time of Operation Flavius, was the Governor of Gibraltar and had authorised the SAS to pursue IRA members. The attack took place on 18 September 1990 at 2100 hours at the Main Road house. The gunman opened fire through a window, hitting Terry, at least nine times and injuring his wife, Betty, near the eye. The couple's daughter, Liz, was found suffering from shock. Terry's face had to be rebuilt as the shots had shattered his face and two high velocity bullets had lodged a fraction of an inch from his brain. Margaret Thatcher later said that she was "utterly appalled and deeply grieved" by the shooting.

Victor Two

The first Gulf war was caused in essence by the Iraqi invasion of Kuwait. The Gulf War started on 2 August 1990. It was caused by the heavy debts incurred by Iraq and the conflict centred around Iraq's claims that Kuwait was Iraqi territory. After the ceasefire with Iran was signed in August 1988, Iraq was heavily debt-ridden. Most of its debt was owed to Saudi Arabia and Kuwait. Iraq pressured both nations to forgive the debts, but they refused. This leads to Saddam Hussein's decision to invade Kuwait.

The operation to remove Saddam Hussein and his army from Kuwait was called 'Operation Desert Storm' and lasted from 17 January to 28 February 1991.

During the first Gulf War, some hundred thousand Iraqi soldiers died. Many were killed by the intense bombing that took place during the war. The SAS was initially tasked with reconnaissance and lazering targets for allied aircraft to bomb. This was followed by hunting for Scud missiles and destroying them. The Scud missiles were a top priority as it was part of a political game to keep Israel out of the war, which would have inflamed various Arab states and potentially enlarged the war. With the Scud threat greatly diminished, the SAS was tasked with attacking a microwave communication station given the target designation of 'Victor Two.' It went on to become one of the largest Special Forces missions undertaken during the war in Iraq. Over half an SAS squadron of men participated, against around 300 Iraqi soldiers.

The previous day, the SAS had identified an Iraqi military position and sent back a report requesting an airstrike. The position was a mobile Scud launcher that needed to be hit before it moved off. Due to the volume of air traffic and reduced availability, it took some time to get a response. SAS command quickly pushed through a strike with some A10 'Warthogs.' These ungainly looking twin-engine aircraft, complete with their GU8-Avenger Gatling gun, rockets and bombs, made short work of the Scud missile and its launcher. Being behind enemy lines meant the SAS were constantly moving, hunting for new targets.

The next day the patrol split up, with three going off to recce a radar installation and the rest to locate an Iraqi airfield. At around midnight, the three SAS troopers found their target of a radar installation. They were about three quarters of a mile away as they sat and observed the

Iraqis. They began to circle the installation to get a better view. While circling the radar installation, they found a fibre optic cable. These were normally buried feet below ground. At the start of the Gulf War, the SBS had been tasked with collecting a sample of cable for intelligence purposes. That successful mission helped secure the utilisation of the SBS and SAS in the Gulf War.

The wire they had found could not easily be destroyed due to its close proximity to the enemy. The other method, which was the one they used, was to dig a hole and place a tow chain round the cable, before using the Land Rover to pull it out. It was a tried and tested method that had caused complete disarray to Iraq communications. With the cable partially destroyed, it was time to bug out of the area before the SAS troopers got caught by an Iraqi patrol. As soon as first light came, it was time to lay low and go into hiding for the day. That night the patrol moved off, but the ground made it hard going for the Land Rovers, with one of them falling down an embankment and trapping two of the lads. One lad was okay, but the other was severely injured and buried under the contents of the Land Rover. The Land Rover was still serviceable and was dragged out of where it had landed before carrying on. The medics patched up the injured SAS trooper before they continued on their journey.

A few days later, a four-vehicle recce patrol was sent out to locate a microwave communication station, undertaking what is called a CTR (Close Target Reconnaissance). They all knew this target would likely be one the SAS would later attack. That night, four Land Rovers made off towards the target. It was hard going, and after two hours of driving they were making slow but sure progress to the target. It was a dreary, overcast night, making navigation difficult even with night vision goggles. The clouds later started to dissipate, giving a glimpse of the stars and enabling much easier navigation.

After three and a half hours of driving, they had still not yet reached their target. The final part of the journey involved crossing an Iraqi motorway. The arena was a hive of activity, with various Iraqi clearance patrols going on around them, most likely looking for suitable positions from which to launch Scud missiles. The problem with crossing the motorway was that the bridge was unsafe and the motorway had a large drainage ditch running down the side of it, which was too deep for the

Land Rovers to cross. They had no choice but to travel a further few miles down a deserted motorway with no lights on, looking for a suitable position to cross. They found a junction and left the motorway. In the distance, the microwave communication centre could clearly be seen, complete with microwave dishes on an antenna surrounded by several buildings. There was a lot of activity at the site and it was a very large installation. The patrol started to head back; as they did so, they noticed that an Iraqi pickup they had spotted earlier had stopped on the motorway and several Iraqi soldiers had jumped out and were walking around the vehicle, which looked like a Toyota Land Cruiser. The SAS patrol stopped and made sure the guns mounted on their Land Rovers could engage the enemy if need be. At this point, it did not look like the Iraqi soldiers had spotted the SAS. The Iraqi soldiers stayed out of their vehicle for approximately five minutes before jumping back in and driving away. The SAS patrol quickly moved away and made it back to base about an hour after daylight.

With the intelligence, and after several messages, a raid on the microwave installation was planned. At 1545 hours, the SAS patrol gathered round a model to receive a briefing and orders. RHQ wanted them to destroy the microwave installation as this was the main control centre guiding the Scud missiles and their launchers. The installation consisted of a building complex with a 200-foot microwave tower. There was a nine-foot internal security fence and 16-foot perimeter wall. Sentries guarded the main gate to the complex. The plan was to drive within a mile of the objective and use the vehicles as fire support. A recce group would go forward, along with close fire support. The recce team would guide the rest of the SAS troopers onto the target, which was to totally destroy the building and its equipment. During the initial attack, two anti-tank missiles would be fired – one missile at the main gate and the other at the sentry position. Explosives would be placed on the inner fence, with the three assault teams affecting entry on the buildings. The building complex had one floor above ground level and two below. Inside, the floors were connected by a central staircase and one assault team was assigned to each floor. Once the Iraqis had been cleared from the building, charges were to be laid. There were believed to be very few military personnel, the majority in the building being civilians, but it was still a dangerous and difficult mission, made more difficult by the SAS already being over 200 miles behind enemy lines.

The patrol commander outlined where the fire support would be positioned and where the assault would start. As soon as that was complete, it was time to prepare for the attack. The final part of the briefing involved the groupings; they were all told, which team they would be on. RHQ had an enormous amount of intelligence on the building, but very little of the enemies' strength.

The afternoon was spent preparing all their kit for the raid, making sure essential equipment was packed and working. At 1830 hours the convoy of vehicles moved out as the darkness and cold set in for the night. After two and a half hours they had reached the main supply route; they held short to make sure there were no Iraqi patrols about before moving into their forward position and splitting up into separate teams. This time, the ditch which had eluded them the night before was filled with several sandbags for the vehicles to drive over. One by one, at a low speed, they crept over the makeshift bridge. Being mobility troop, they had created such bridges in training many times before, but it is always different doing it under battle conditions behind enemy lines. As they got close to the objective, a series of man-made trenches dug in long lines meant the vehicles had to detour slightly before finally coming to their forward position about a mile from their objective.

After doing a recce on the objective, it became clear that there were quite a few vehicles and personnel milling about. It was decided to drive in closer, and it was not long before they hit the main entrance road and began to drive down it, past slit trenches with Iraqi soldiers in them. Further along, the convoy of eight vehicles pulled up against a small escarpment that ran alongside the road. The SAS was now in the middle of a large enemy position, trying to formulate a new plan. With a new plan of action, the team moved off and parked up behind a large sand bank about 200 yards from the objective.

The tower and its control buildings were surrounded by a wall, behind which would be the second perimeter fence as described in their briefing. It was now easy to determine the damage to the buildings that various bombing missions had done, but not successfully destroyed. A lead scout was sent in to give an early warning to the rest of the team. As the lead scout moved forward, more detail of the objective came into view. As they moved up towards a road, they held short and went into all-round defence. They would need to cross a road and move over open ground to make it to the objective. They headed back to the rest of the SAS team to report their findings. With this further information on the target it was decided to utilise the vehicles to give flank protection, while the main group, consisting of the demolition teams and fire support, moved up towards the main tower.

They quickly came upon another slit trench covered in a tin sheet, but this was empty so the team pushed forward, before noticing a pile of sandbags in a corner that looked like another enemy position. This position was also empty, so they continued forward another few hundred feet. They were very nearly spotted by a bus, but they dived behind some rocks just in time. Two of the team went back to get the vehicles moved forward before returning to the assault team. Nearby, a fuel truck complete with a browser would serve as a good observation position.

The demolition team started their move towards their assigned objectives as the fire support team got into position. There was an almost eerie silence that made everything seem a bit too calm. The silence was interrupted by a mumbling coming from inside the cab of the truck. The cab contained a young Iraqi soldier of about sixteen years and another Iraqi soldier, both fast asleep. They were soon awoken by the two SAS soldiers, who had no choice but to kill them. Two short bursts of fire riddled the cab with bullets and both the Iraqi soldiers lay dead. The noise of gunfire awoke the Iraqi defences and almost instantaneously, small arms fire opened up followed by Russian SU22 anti-aircraft guns. Red and green tracer rounds were now whizzing across the sky, before ricocheting or impacting the ground. The fire was completely random and it was obvious the Iraqis had no idea where the SAS were. The SAS was now compromised and there was little point remaining stealthy. The demolition teams were busy planting their charges, although the stealth bombers had done a pretty good job and had badly damaged the control centre already.

Small arms fire was coming from all directions as the four charges were placed on the microwave tower. As soon as they were placed, the small grip switches were depressed, giving them a minute and 30 seconds to get a safe distance away. The assault team prepared to leave, but one entrance was blocked by tracer fire. They had no choice but to run the gauntlet, as in less than a minute the microwave tower would come crashing down on them. The team ran like mad to find cover, and luckily no one was hit. Only three of the four charges went off, but this was enough to cause the column to buckle and crash down to the ground, accompanied by a shower of dust and debris. After the detonation, the enemy fire seemed to become more intense, but was only partially effective. The SAS team quickly got into formation and began their retreat from the area. As they drew close to their vehicles, three Iraqi soldiers opened up on them, hitting one of the SAS soldiers through the trouser leg. Confusion led to one vehicle speeding away into the night as the SAS tried to get organised.

The fire support group also needed to withdraw. What was not known at the time was that there were still some SAS soldiers at the actual objective, desperately making their way back. It was going to be a slow fighting retreat as thousands of rounds buzzed all round them. The fire support group and their vehicles joined up with the rest of the SAS soldiers. They now had to punch their way through the various slit trenches and Iraqi soldiers before they could finally get away into the night and relative safety of the desert. Victor Two was a very successful and classic SAS mission. Reconnaissance the next day showed that all the masts had been destroyed and the facility put out of action. No injuries were sustained by the SAS either, which is all the more amazing due to the amount of sustained fire the Iraqis poured onto the SAS.

Operation Gothic Serpent

Operation Gothic Serpent was an operation conducted in Somalia in the 1990s by United States special operations forces with the primary mission of capturing warlord Mohamed Farrah Aidid. The operation occurred in Somalia from August to October 1993 and was supervised by the Joint Special Operations Command (JSOC). As part of the operation, the soldiers were deployed to arrest two of Aidid's lieutenants. The mission was part of Gothic Serpent and became the battle of Mogadishu to those involved in it.

The start of the Somalian problem began in 1991 during a time of great change. The Barre administration was ousted that year by a coalition of clan-based opposition groups, backed by Ethiopia's then-ruling Derg regime and Libya. Following a meeting of the Somali National Movement and northern clan elders, the northern former British portion of the country declared its independence as Somaliland in May 1991. Although de facto independent and relatively stable compared to the tumultuous south, it has not been recognized by any foreign government. Prior to the civil war, Mogadishu was known as the "White pearl of the Indian Ocean"

Many of the opposition groups subsequently began competing for influence in the power vacuum that followed the removal of Barre's regime. In the south, armed factions led by USC commanders, General Mohamed Farah Aidid and Ali Mahdi Mohamed, in particular, clashed as each sought to exert authority over the capital. In 1991, a multi-phased international conference on Somalia was held in neighbouring Djibouti. Aidid boycotted the first meeting in protest. Due to the legitimacy conferred on Muhammad by the Djibouti conference, he was subsequently recognized by the international community as the new President of Somalia. Djibouti, Egypt, Saudi Arabia and Italy were among the countries that officially extended recognition to Muhammad's administration. However, he was not able to exert his authority beyond parts of the capital. Power was instead vied with other faction leaders in the southern half of the country and with autonomous subnational entities in the north.

UN Security Council Resolution 733 and UN Security Council Resolution 746 led to the creation of UNOSOM I, the first mission to provide humanitarian relief and help restore order in Somalia after the dissolution of its central government. United Nations Security Council Resolution 794 was unanimously passed on 3 December 1992, which approved a coalition of United Nations peacekeepers led by the United States. Forming the Unified Task Force (UNITAF), the alliance was tasked with assuring security until humanitarian efforts aimed at stabilizing the situation were transferred to the UN. Landing in 1993, the UN peacekeeping coalition started the two-year United Nations Operation in Somalia II (UNOSOM II) primarily in the south. UNITAF's original mandate was to use "all necessary means" to guarantee the delivery of humanitarian aid in accordance to Chapter VII of the United Nations Charter, and is regarded as a success.

In December 1992, U.S. President George H. W. Bush ordered the U.S. military to join the UN in a joint operation known as Operation Restore Hope, with the primary mission of restoring order in Somalia. The country was wracked by civil war and a severe famine as it was ruled by a number of warlords. Over the next several months, the situation deteriorated and greater intervention became a necessity.

In May 1993, all the parties involved in the civil war agreed to a disarmament conference proposed by the leading Somali warlord, Mohamed Farrah Aidid. The Somali National Alliance had been formed in June 1992. This alliance consisted of warlords across the country, operating under Aidid's authority, Aidid having declared himself Somalia's president. A great number of Somali civilians also resented the international forces, leading many, including women and children, to take up arms and actively resist U.S. forces during fighting in Mogadishu. On 5 June 1993, one of the deadliest attacks on UN forces in Somalia occurred when 24 Pakistani soldiers were ambushed and killed in an Aidid-controlled area of Mogadishu.

Any hope of a peaceful resolution of the conflict quickly vanished. The next day, the UN's Security Council issued Resolution 837, calling for the arrest and trial of the ambush's perpetrators. U.S. warplanes and UN troops began an attack on Aidid's stronghold. Aidid remained defiant, and the violence between Somalis and UN forces escalated. On 8 August 1993, Aidid's militia detonated a remote controlled bomb against a U.S. military vehicle, killing four soldiers. Two weeks later, another bomb injured another seven U.S. soldiers. In response, President Clinton, who had taken up office on 20 January 1993, approved the proposal to deploy a special task force, composed of 400 U.S. Delta Force commandos and Army Rangers. This unit, named Task Force Ranger, consisted of 160 elite U.S. troops. They flew to Mogadishu and began a manhunt for Aidid. Task Force Ranger was deployed on 22 August 1993 to Somalia under the command of Major General William F. Garrison, JSOC's commander at the time. It consisted of B Company, 3rd Battalion, 75th Ranger Regiment, C Squadron, 1st Special Forces Operational Detachment-Delta (1st SFOD-D). As well as the main force, 16 helicopters and personnel from the 160th Special Operations Aviation Regiment -160th SOAR, which included MH-60 Black Hawks and AH/MH-6 helicopters. From the Naval Special Warfare Development Group (DEVGRU) some US Navy SEALs. Air Force Pararescuemen and Combat Controllers from the 24th Special Tactics Squadron.

The task force occupied an old hangar and construction trailers just outside of Mogadishu under primitive conditions. The force lacked potable water and was subject to frequent mortar fire due to its proximity to the main part of Mogadishu. During September, the force conducted several successful missions to arrest Aidid's sympathizers and to confiscate arms caches. Helicopters made frequent flights over the city to desensitize the public to the presence of military aircraft and to familiarize themselves with the city's narrow streets and alleys. However, these same flights allowed Aidid's followers to calculate how they could be shot down.

On 21 September, the force captured Aidid's financier, Osman Ali Atto, when a Delta team intercepted a vehicle convoy transporting him out of the city. At around 0200 hours on 25 September, Aidid's men shot down a Black Hawk with RPG and killed three of the crew members at New Port near Mogadishu. Although the helicopter was not part of a Task Force Ranger mission, the Black Hawk destruction was a major victory for Aidid's forces.

On Sunday, 3 October 1993, Task Force Ranger, U.S. special operations forces composed mainly of Bravo Company 3rd Battalion, 75th Ranger Regiment, 1st Special Forces Operational Delta Force operators, and the 160th Special Operations Aviation Regiment, also known as "The Night Stalkers," attempted to capture Aidid's foreign minister Omar Salad Elmi and his top political advisor, Mohamed Hassan Awale.

The plan was that Delta operators would assault the target building (using MH-6 Little Bird helicopters) and secure the targets inside the building while four Ranger chalks would fast rope down from hovering MH-60L Black Hawk helicopters. The Rangers would create a four-corner, defensive perimeter around the building while a column of nine Humvee's and three M939 five-ton trucks would arrive at the building to take the entire assault team and their prisoners back to base. The entire operation was estimated to take no longer than 30 minutes.

At 1350 hours, Task Force Ranger analysts receive intelligence of Salad's location. At 1542 hours, the MH-6 assault Little Birds carrying the Delta operators hit the target, the wave of dust becoming so bad that one was forced to go around again and land out of position. Two Black Hawks followed, carrying the second Delta assault team, moved into position and dropped their teams as the four Ranger chalks prepared to rope onto the four corners surrounding the target building. By mistake, Chalk Four being carried by Black Hawk callsign Super 67, was accidentally put in a block north of their intended point. Declining the pilot's offer to move them back down due to the time it would take to do so, leaving the helicopter too exposed, Chalk Four intended to move down to the planned position, but intense ground fire prevented them from doing so.

The task force for the operation had sent in 19 aircraft, 12 vehicles, and 160 men to arrest them. Most of which was needed to secure the area directly after the arrest, as Aidid's force would quickly swarm into the area. During the mission, Private Todd Blackburn missed the rope while fast-roping from an MH-60 Black Hawk helicopter, when he fell 70 feet to the street below, seriously wounding himself. The two Somali leaders were quickly located ad arrested before loaded on a convoy of ground vehicles along with the seriously wounded Private Blackburn. The ground-extraction convoy was supposed to reach the captive targets a few minutes after the operation's beginning. However, it ran into delays as Somali citizens and local militia formed barricades along Mogadishu's streets with rocks, wreckage, rubbish and burning tires. Blocking the convoy from easily reaching the Rangers and their captives. Aidid militiamen with megaphones were shouting, "Come out and defend your homes!"

Sergeant Dominick Pilla and a Somali combatant spotted each other and fired at the same time. Both were killed in the short exchange of fire. The operation's commanders were stunned to hear that a soldier had been killed, as they expected no casualties during the operation. During the battle's first hours, the MH-60 Black Hawk, Super Six One, piloted by Cliff Wolcott, was shot down by a Somali combatant using a RPG. The pilots were killed during the crash landing, but the crew survived.

A while Later, another Black Hawk, Super Six Four, was also shot down by an RPG fired from the ground. No rescue team was immediately available to go in and get them out of a very scary and dangerous situation. The small surviving crew, including one of the pilots, Michael Durant, couldn't move. Two Delta snipers — Master Sergeant Gary Gordon and Sergeant First Class Randy Shughart provided cover from a helicopter flying in small circles from above. Both of them repeatedly volunteered to secure the crash site. After three requests, they were given permission to go in, however, they were fully aware this offer of support would mean they would more than likely pay with their lives. As soon as they arrived at the crash site, they attempted to secure the site and in the process Master Sergeant Gordon was killed, leaving only Durant and Shughart. Eventually, after holding off and killing more than 25 Somalis, Shughart was also killed and their position was overrun. Durant was taken hostage after beating him violently. Many of those in the mob were high on drugs, meaning the situation was even more dangerous and frightening. Drugs often mask pain and increase aggression levels. The mob who attacked Durant acted more like a pack of wolves with its prey. Durant was released after 11 days of captivity.

At the same time the remaining Rangers and Delta Force operators were fighting their way to the first crash site, where they found the crew. They soon found themselves surrounded by Somali Habr Gidr militia. The Somali commander, Colonel Sharif Hassan Giumale, decided to kill the U.S. troops with mortar fire, and Somali militia prepared to bombard the pinned down Americans with 60mm mortars, which would have wiped out the soldiers and anyone else in quite close proximity. However, Colonel Giumale called off the mortar strike after information of possible civilian hostages arose. Repeated attempts by the Somalis to overrun U.S. positions were beaten back with heavy small arms fire accompanied by strafing and rocket fire from helicopters that tried their best to suppress the attacking militia. A rescue convoy was organised, made up of the U.S. Army's 10th Mountain Division along with Malaysian and Pakistani forces. They had to break through a very well secured perimeter and fight trough, whilst taking very heavy fire from the militia. It has become one of the most intensive close quarter battles that US forces have encountered since the Vietnam War.

The battle was over by 0630 hours on 4 October 1993. U.S. forces were finally evacuated to the UN base by the armoured convoy sent in to rescue them. While leaving the crash site, a group of Rangers and Delta operators realised that there was no room left in the vehicles. This meant they had no choice but to depart the city on foot to an RV on National Street. This has been commonly referred to as the "Mogadishu Mile".

In all, 18 U.S. soldiers were killed in action during the battle and another 73 were wounded in action. The Malaysian forces lost one soldier and had seven injured, while the Pakistanis suffered two injured. Two MH-60 Black Hawks were shot down, another was seriously damaged. Somali casualties were heavy, with estimates on fatalities ranging from 315 to over 2,000 combatants. The Somali casualties were a mixture of militiamen and local civilians. Somali civilians suffered heavy casualties due to the dense urban character of that portion of Mogadishu.

Two weeks after the battle, General Garrison officially accepted responsibility. In a handwritten letter to President Clinton, Garrison took full responsibility for the battle's outcome. He wrote that Task Force Ranger had adequate intelligence for the mission and that their objective, capturing targets from the Olympic Hotel was met.

The battle turned out to be the most intensive close combat that U.S. troops had engaged in since the Vietnam War. The mission objective of capturing Aidid's associates was also accomplished. But the high price in terms of casualties on both sides. It was not an end to the violence, when two days after the battle's end, Somali militiamen launched a mortar strike on a U.S. compound and Delta operator Sergeant First Class Matt Rierson was killed. After the battle, the bodies of several of the conflict's U.S. casualties from the Black Hawk Super 64's and their defenders, Delta Force soldiers Gordon and Shughart were dragged through Mogadishu's streets by crowds of local civilians and SNA forces. All their equipment and much of their clothing was removed. Through negotiation and threats to the Habr Gidr clan leaders by ambassador

Robert B. Oakley, all the bodies were eventually recovered. The bodies were returned in a terrible condition, with horrific post mortem injuries cause by the mob, one with a severed head.

Following the battle, President Clinton ordered that additional troops be added to protect U.S. soldiers and aid in withdrawal. All military actions were ceased on October 6, except in cases of self-defence. Clinton called for a full withdrawal by 31 March 1994. Conforming to this request, most troops were out of the country by 25 March 1994. A few hundred U.S. Marines remained offshore, but were completely removed from the area by March 1995.

With the withdrawal of the UN, Aidid subsequently declared himself President of Somalia in June 1995. However, his declaration received no recognition, as his rival Ali Mahdi Muhammad had already been elected interim President at a conference in Djibouti and recognised as such by the international community. Consequently, Aidid's faction continued its quest for his own form of indirect government in the south. During September 1995, militia forces loyal to him attacked the city of Baidoa, killing 10 local residents and capturing at least 20 foreign aid workers.

Aidid died on 24 July 1996, when Aidid and his men clashed with forces of former allies Ali Mahdi Muhammad and Osman Ali Atto. Aidid suffered a gunshot wound during the battle. He later died from a heart attack on 1 August 1996, it is unsure if this was during or after surgery.

Between 31 May and 9 June 2008, representatives of Somalia's federal government and the moderate Alliance for the Re-liberation of Somalia (ARS) group of Islamist rebels participated in peace talks in Djibouti brokered by the UN. The conference ended with a signed agreement calling for the withdrawal of Ethiopian troops in exchange for the cessation of armed confrontation. Parliament was subsequently expanded to 550 seats to accommodate ARS members, who elected a new president. With the help of a small team of African Union troops, the coalition government also began a counteroffensive in February 2009 to retake control of the southern half of the country. To solidify its control of southern Somalia, the TFG formed an alliance with the Islamic Courts Union, other members of the Alliance for the Re-liberation of Somalia, and Ahlu Sunna Waljama'a, a moderate Sufi militia.

In November 2010, a new technocratic government was elected to office, which enacted numerous reforms, especially in the security sector.

By August 2011, the new administration and its AMISOM allies had managed to capture all of Mogadishu from the Al-Shabaab militants. Mogadishu has subsequently experienced a period of intense reconstruction spearheaded by the Somali diaspora, the municipal authorities, and Turkey, an historic ally of Somalia.

Operation Tango

The war in Bosnia became an international conflict involving forces from around the world. The war lasted from 1 March 1992 to 14 December 1995. It involved several factions and was mainly a territorial conflict. The main elements involved were the forces of the self-proclaimed Bosnian Serb and Bosnian Croat entities within Bosnia and Herzegovina, the Republic of Bosnia and Herzegovina and those of the Republika Srpska and Herzeg-Bosnia.

The war came about as a result of the break-up of Yugoslavia. Following the Slovenian and Croatian secessions from the Socialist Federal Republic of Yugoslavia in 1991, the multi-ethnic Socialist Republic of Bosnia and Herzegovina, which was inhabited by 44% Muslim Bosniaks, 31% Orthodox Serbs and 17% Catholic Croats, passed a referendum for independence on 29 February 1992. This was rejected by the Bosnian Serbs' political representatives who had boycotted the referendum. After the declaration of independence, the Bosnian Serbs, who were backed by the Serbian government and Yugoslav People's Army, made sure that Serbian Territory was secure. War broke out across the country and the ethnic cleansing of the Muslim Bosniak population began. Ethnic cleansing quickly became a common phenomenon in the war. It typically entailed intimidation, forced expulsion and more often than not, the killing of the undesired ethnic group. Alongside this was the destruction or removal of the physical vestiges of the ethnic group, such as places of worship, cemeteries and cultural and historical buildings. At the end of the war, various leaders were wanted for war crimes and had to be tracked down and brought in for justice.

On 10 July, 1997, a ten-man SAS team was deployed in the forested mountains surrounding the Bosnian Serb capital of Pale. They had been brought in by Chinook helicopters to begin Operation Tango. The operation involved the detention of Simo Drljaca and Milan Kovacevic by an SAS team in the area of Prijedor, north-west Bosnia. Intelligence services had already been following them for some time and making sure they were the correct target. The SAS moved in to capture Drljaca, a former police chief suspected of orchestrating the ethnic cleansing of Prijedor's Muslim population. He was also suspected of helping other suspected war criminals by providing fake documents and safe houses.

The SAS carried indictments issued by the International Criminal Tribunal for the Former Yugoslavia. Drljaca was approached on a road outside the town as part of a fishing party at Prijedor reservoir. Drljaca had no intention of coming quietly and fired his pistol. He hit one of the SAS soldiers in the leg, before the rest of the SAS team opened fire and killed him. The other three people with him were arrested and later released without charge. The Drljaca's body was taken by an American helicopter to its base in Tuzla. The shot SAS soldier was only slightly injured.

The second target, Kovacevic, did not offer resistance and was arrested at Prijedor hospital, where he was the director. Kovacevic was the mayor of Prijedor in 1992. He was suspected of organising the roundup of Muslims for interment in the notorious camps at Omarska, Keraterm and Trnopolje, where many were reportedly beaten and starved to death. At about 9:30am on 10 July 1997, the SAS team moved in. They talked their way into the hospital by posing as Red Cross officials, hiding their 9mm pistols beneath their clothing. The SAS promptly arrested Kovacevic, who did not resist. Kovacevic was flown by helicopter to the American base at Tuzla, where Drljaca's body had also been taken. From there he was airlifted by C130 to The Hague to face trial. Kovacevic died of a heart attack whilst in custody a year later on 1 August 1998.

In light of the first successful operation, a similar mission was planned five months later. In support of continued international efforts to bring Bosnian war crimes suspects to justice, Dutch and British Special Forces arrested two Bosnian Croats in the central Bosnian town of Vitez, 30 miles northwest of Sarajevo. Vlatko Kupreskic, 39, and Anto Furundzija, 28, were apprehended at their homes in simultaneous operations in the early morning hours of 18 December 1997. Once caught, they were transported to The Hague in the Netherlands to face formal indictment by the United Nations International War Crimes Tribunal.

To arrest both Kupreskic and Furundzija, a small team of Dutch commandos from the 108th Special Forces Company were inserted by helicopter not far from the town of Vitez. The team joined SAS soldiers who were already operating in Bosnia. In pairs, the Dutch commandos set up covert OPs (Observation Posts) near the suspects' homes and carried out surveillance so they could establish patterns or movement. Immediately prior to the arrest of Kupresikic, telephone lines to his home were severed and the family's night watchman was tied up and gagged. Once the exterior had been secured, a dynamic entry into the home was conducted using an explosive device at the front door, followed by tear gas and stun grenades. Nonetheless, these diversionary tools were not completely effective, Kupreskic managed to grab an automatic weapon and engage the Special Forces. In the brief fire fight that followed, Kupreskic was wounded in the arm, shoulder, and leg, without any injuries being sustained by the assault team.

The arrest of Furundzija was carried out in a different section of Vitez and was very close to being aborted after surveillance observed him driving past his home shortly after midnight. This led to fears that the mission had been somehow compromised. Nevertheless, he circled back and turned back to his home. Upon entering his house, he was challenged by Special Forces and arrested, offering no resistance. It was determined after questioning that Furundzija was intoxicated, he had simply missed the driveway to his house and had compromised.

Officials voiced some concern over the threat of reprisals by Bosnian Serbs resentful of NATO arrest attempts. Following Operation Tango, an unidentified individual threw four grenades into a British military outpost, causing minor damage but no casualties. It was later speculated that the incident had been perpetrated by a member of the Bosnian Serb special police force serving in a bodyguard unit for senior officials and VIPs. These units had been largely banned by NATO, but many members retained their weapons and equipment. The only protests stemming from the 18 December Dutch-led operation came in the form of temporary roadblocks constructed by local citizens on the roads leading into and out of the town of Vitez. These were mostly peaceful in nature and no direct actions were taken against NATO forces in the country.

Operation Chavin du Huanter

The ambush and seizure of the Japanese ambassador's residency on December 17, 1996 in Lima, Peru came as a complete surprise and was the highest profile operation of the Túpac Amaru Revolutionary Movement (MRTA) in its 15-year history. The MRTA was a South American Revolutionary Alliance protest movement active in South America from the early 1900s and ongoing today as a centre left part and one of the main actors in the International poverty conflict in South America. One of its leaders was Víctor Polay Campos, who was the son of Chinese immigrant Victor Polay Risco until he was tortured and incarcerated for 32 years. One of the other leaders was Néstor Cerpa Cartolini until his death in 1997 during. The MRTA took its name in part as a tribute to Túpac Amaru II, an 18th century rebel leader who was himself named after his ancestor Túpac Amaru, the last indigenous leader of the Inca people. MRTA was considered a terrorist organization by the Peruvian government, the US Department of State and the European Parliament. At the height of its strength, the movement had several hundred active members. Their goal was to establish a socialist state in Peru.

The attack by the MRTA propelled Peru in general, and the MRTA in particular, into the world spotlight for the duration of the crisis. Guests of the Japanese ambassador, reported that the MRTA guerrillas blasted a hole in the garden wall of the Japanese ambassador's residence at around 2020 hours on the December 17, 1996. The complex had been guarded by over 300 heavily armed police officers and bodyguards. The Japanese ambassador's residence had been converted into a fortress by the Japanese government. It was surrounded by a 12-foot wall, bars on all windows, bullet-proof glass in many windows and doors that were built to withstand the impact of a grenade. This made it an ideal target to use as a fortress for defence purposes.

The news of the MRTA's daring assault on the ambassador's residence caused the Lima Stock Exchange to close three hours early, as domestic stocks plummeted. The news came during a period of low popularity for President Fujimori or popularity had fallen from 75% to 40%. He had, up until that point been credited with restoring peace to the country after terrorist activity largely ceased in Peru during his first presidential term.

On 22 December 1996, Fujimori made his first public announcement on the hostage-taking. In a televised four-minute speech he condemned the assailants, calling the MRTA assault "repugnant" and rejecting all of the MRTA's demands. He did not rule out an armed rescue attempt, but said that he was willing to explore a peaceful solution to end the situation. He also publicly indicated that he did not need help from foreign security advisors, following speculation circulated that Peru was turning to foreign governments for assistance. He knew that it was important for both his presidency and Peru, to take control of the situation without outside support, showing Peru's strength and resilience to terrorism.

In the days after the Japanese Embassy had been taken, the International Committee of the Red Cross acted as an intermediary between the government and members of the MRTA. Among the hostages were high officials of Peru's security forces, including Máximo Rivera, the chief of Peru's anti-terrorist police, DIRCOTE, and former chief Carlos Domínguez. Other hostages included Alejandro Toledo, who later became President of Peru, and Javier Diez Canseco, a socialist politician, Peruvian congressman. The 24 Japanese hostages included President Fujimori's own mother and younger brother. The leader of the MRTA insurgents was identified as 43-year old Néstor Cerpa.

Fujimori had made his speech shortly after MRTA leader Cerpa announced that he would gradually release any hostages who were not connected to the Peruvian government. During the months of the siege that followed, the rebels released all female hostages and all but 72 of the men. The MRTA's demands were the release of their members from prisons around Peru, including a recently convicted US activist Lori Berenson and also Cerpa's wife, a revision of the government's neoliberal free market reforms. The MRTA also singled out Japan's foreign assistance program in Peru for criticism, arguing that this aid benefited only a narrow segment of society. Their final protest was against the claimed cruel and inhumane conditions in Peru's jails.

Leftist politician Javier Diez Canseco was among the 38 men who were released very shortly after the hostages were taken. He defended the MRTA and called for the government to negotiate a settlement. Diez Canseco said that the hostage-takers are between an 18 and maybe 21 years of age. He went on to say that he did not believe that the group wished to lose their lives.

Upon being freed, Alejandro Toledo said that what the MRTA really wanted was an amnesty, which would allow its members to participate freely in public life. He said that any attempt to rescue the hostages by force would be difficult as they were all heavily armed. Toledo also said that rooms in the building were wired with explosives, as well as the roof. He added that the terrorists had anti-tank weapons and wore backpacks that were filled with explosives, which could be detonated by pulling a cord on their chest.

With Fujimori, wanting a peaceful solution if possible, he appointed a team to hold talks with the MRTA, including the Canadian ambassador, Anthony Vincent, who had briefly been a hostage, Archbishop Juan Luis Cipriani, and a Red Cross official. Fujimori even talked with the Cuban leader Fidel Castro, raising media speculation that a deal was being worked out to let the MRTA involved go to Cuba as political exiles. However, on 17 January, negotiations with the MRTA had stalled.

In early February 1997, a new squad of Peruvian troops with heavy equipment took over the embassy overwatch. They played loud military music and made provocative gestures to the rebels, who unleashed a burst of gunfire. This prompted the Prime Minister of Japan, Ryutaro Hashimoto, to publicly urge Peru to refrain from taking any unnecessary risks that could endanger the hostages' lives. Japanese leaders pressured Fujimori to reach some sort of negotiated settlement with the Tupac Amaru rebels in order to ensure the hostages' safe release. Fujimori met Hashimoto in Canada. The two leaders announced that they were in agreement on how to handle the hostage situation, but provided few details as they did not want media publicity which could have blown any operation.

On 10 February 1997, Fujimori travelled to London, where he announced that the purpose of his trip was to "find a country that would give asylum to the MRTA group". Observers noted that his request that the MRTA group be given political asylum contradicted his previously-stated position that the MRTA were not guerrillas but terrorists. On 11 February Fujimori declared that "Peruvian prisons are built in accordance with international standards for terrorists." He also attended business meetings, which he described to his domestic audience as an "exercise in reassuring the international investors."

All the while the Peruvian government via the Army Intelligence Agency had a plan if intervention and a military operation was required. The plan was said to involve the direct participation of U.S. military forces. The Special Forces involved would come from the Peruvian Army's School of Commandos and the United States Southern Command, based in Panama. The MRTA called off the talks with the government in March when they reported hearing loud noises coming from beneath the floor of the residence. Peruvian newspapers confirmed the MRTA suspicions, reporting that the police were digging tunnels underneath the building. The police tried to cover up noise from the digging by playing loud music over loudspeakers and carrying out noisy tank manoeuvres through the nearby streets. Military intervention was becoming a reality. In preparation for the raid, one of the hostages, Peruvian Navy Admiral Luis Giampietri, who was an expert on intelligence and command operations, was secretly provided with a miniature two-way radio set and given encrypted instructions to warn the hostages ten minutes before the military operation began, telling them to stay as far away as possible from the MRTA members. Light coloured clothes were sent in bit by bit for the hostages, so that they could be distinguished easily from the dark-clad insurgents during the planned raid. Cerpa himself unwittingly helped with this part of the project when, hearing noise that made him suspect that a tunnel was being dug, he ordered all the hostages placed on the second floor, keeping them more centralised and making any rescue attempt a little bit more straight forward.

In addition, sophisticated miniature microphones and video cameras had been smuggled into the residence, concealed in books, water bottles, and table games. Giampietri and other military officers among the hostages were given the responsibility for placing these devices in secure locations around the house. Eavesdropping on the MRTA with the help of these high-tech devices, military planners observed that the insurgents had organised their security carefully, and were particularly alert during the night hours. However, early every afternoon, eight of the MRTA members, including the four leaders, played indoor football for about one hour. Being able to gather intelligence, such as this, was crucial to any successful rescue mission against heavily armed and determined group, which had months in which to secure and prepare for any required attack against them.

The Peruvians made a scale model to aid in preparation for the rescue operation. The model included the tunnels from adjacent houses.

On 22 April 1997, more than four months after the beginning of the siege, a team of 140 Peruvian commandos, assembled into a secret ad-hoc unit given the name Chavín de Huantar. This was a reference to a Peruvian archaeological site famous for its underground passageways. They were to mount a dramatic raid on the Japanese embassy.

In the afternoon of the 22 April at 1523 hours, Operation Chavín de Huántar began with three explosive charges exploding almost simultaneously in three different rooms on the first floor. The first explosion hit in the middle of the room where the soccer game was taking place, killing three of the MRTA immediately, two of the men and one of the women. Through the hole created by that blast and the other two explosions, 30 commandos stormed into the building, chasing the surviving MRTA members in order to stop them before they could reach the second floor and most likely start killing hostages.

Two other moves were made simultaneously with the explosions. In the first, 20 commandos launched a direct assault on the front door, in order to join their comrades inside the waiting room, where the main staircase to the second floor was located. On their way in, they found the two female MRTA's guarding the front door. Behind the first wave of commandos storming the door came another group of soldiers carrying ladders, which they placed against the rear walls of the building.

In the final part of the coordinated attack, another group of commandos emerged from two tunnels that had reached the back yard of the residence. These soldiers quickly scaled the ladders that had been placed for them. Their tasks were to blow out a grenade proof door on the second floor, through which the hostages could be evacuated. They were also to make two openings in the roof so that they could kill the MRTA upstairs before they had any time to execute the hostages.

By the end of the operation, all 14 MRTA guerrillas, one hostage and two soldiers, Lieutenant Colonel Juan Valer Sandoval and Lieutenant Raúl Jiménez Chávez were dead. It was a fierce firefight, but the coordinated attack and planning at ad gone into the operation paid off, with the low loss of life outside of the MRTA.

One MRTA member Roli Rojas was discovered attempting to walk out of the residency mixed with the hostages. A commando spotted him and dragged him out before taking him to the back of the house executing him with a burst of fire that blew off Rojas' head as the commando had intended to fire a single shot to the head instead of a burst of fire. Fujimori personally ordered the commandos participating in the raid to "take no MRTA alive." However, with the heavy firepower the MRTA had, and their willingness to stand and fight as opposed to surrendering, this was not an easy option in the heat of battle.

As the commandos tore down the flag of the MRTA that had been flying on the roof of the embassy, Fujimori joined some of the former hostages in singing the Peruvian national anthem. Peruvian TV also showed Fujimori striding among the dead MRTA; some of the bodies were mutilated. Fujimori was famously photographed standing over the bodies of Nestor Cerpa and Roli Rojas on the main staircase of the residence, and Rojas' destroyed head is noticeable in the photograph.

When the operation was over, the bodies of the MRTA dead, were removed by military prosecutors; representatives from the Attorney General's Office were not permitted entry. The corpses were not taken to the Institute of Forensic Medicine for autopsy as required by law. Rather, the bodies were taken to the morgue at the Police Hospital. It was there that the autopsies were performed. The autopsy reports were kept secret until 2001. Next of kin of the deceased were not allowed to be present for the identification of the bodies and the autopsies. Eligia Rodríguez Bustamante, the mother of one of the guerrillas, and the Deputy Director of APRODEH asked the Attorney General's Office to take the necessary steps to identify those who died during the rescue, but the Attorney General's Office conceded its jurisdiction over the identity of the deceased MRTA members to the military justice system. The bodies of the MRTA killed in the operation were buried in secrecy in cemeteries throughout Lima.

Shortly after the operation, President Fujimori was seen riding through Lima on a bus carrying the freed hostages. This was mainly a PR exercise to aid in Fujimori popularity and as a visible reminder as the potential fate for any other would be terrorists and bolster his hard-line stance against armed insurgent groups.

Fujimori popularity ratings quickly doubled to nearly 70 percent, and he was acclaimed a national hero. The operation was so successful that there was no opposition to it. Reflecting on the raid a few days afterwards, Antonio Cisneros, a leading poet, said it had given Peruvians a little bit of dignity. Nobody expected this efficiency, this speed. In military terms it was a First World job, not a Third World. An operation to match other world class special forces operations. The Peruvian assault team had been trained by American Special Forces, with support provided by Delta Force during the operation. Six members of the British SAS were also present, due to diplomatic personnel being among the hostages. The SAS where possible like to at least be observers, in many different operations around the world, as there is much to be learnt from any operation. Be it be either a success or failure, as this can be incorporated in further training or planning of other operations.

Operation Barras

Sierra Leone is in West Africa, bordered by Guinea to the northeast, Liberia to the southeast, and the Atlantic Ocean to the southwest. The country's economy is largely based on mining and it is one of the largest producers of titanium and bauxite, the principal source of aluminium. Between 1991 and 2001, the country was gripped in a rebellion to overthrow the regime that had negated on its promise of political reform. In October 1999, the UN established the United Nations Mission in Sierra Leone (UNAMSIL). The main objective of UNAMSIL was to assist with the disarmament process and enforce the terms established under the Lome Peace Agreement.

It was late summer 2000 in Sierra Leone, when a group of Royal Irish Rangers in their WMIK (Weapons Mount Installation Kit) Land Rovers made their way along a dusty track surrounded by fairly dense jungle vegetation. Sierra Leone used to be a British Colony and is roughly the size of Scotland. The patrol veered off the main road and onto a small track, heading towards the village of Magbeni, after being told over lunch that the West Side Boys had begun to disarm. The Irish Rangers were part of the United Nations peacekeeping force out in Sierra Leone. The Irish Rangers Land Rovers were heavily armed and they had no reason to be any more alert than usual on a patrol. The patrol came to a standstill when a Bedford lorry, on which was mounted an anti-aircraft gun, blocked their path. A group of West Side Boys leapt out from the foliage either side of the WMIKs and quickly surrounded them. Major Marshall dismounted his WIMIK and approached; as he did so, one of the West Side Boys tried to grab his weapon and he got into a tussle, refusing to let it go. For that he received a beating, and realising the situation, the rest of the patrol became compliant. The Irish Rangers had no choice but to surrender their weapons and be taken hostage by the West Side Boys, who took the captured WMIKs and soldiers back to their base before putting out a ransom demand and some concessions. The soldiers were placed in canoes and taken back to the West Side Boys' base at Geri Bana, a short distance from the village of Magbeni, which the West Side Boys also controlled.

The West Side Boys were sometimes depicted as a splinter faction of the Armed Forces Revolutionary Council. They were a heavily-armed group, known for their fearlessness and ruthlessness. Many had served in the Sierra Leone Army and had refused to integrate into the reconstituted army. In many ways, they were influenced by gangster rap music, especially that of Tupac. They wore flamboyant clothing, often with flip flops and women's wigs. At their peak, they were about 600 strong.

Once they were back at their base, they sent out their initial demands. The negotiations were conducted by Lieutenant Colonel Simon Fordham, who was aided by a small team which included hostage negotiators from the Metropolitan Police force. Initially, the negotiations went well. Four days after the seizure of the Irish Rangers on 29 August, Fordham demanded to know that all the Irish Rangers were safe and well. He was met by the West Side Boys' leader, Foday Kallay, who brought with him Major Marshall and Captain Flaherty. When Flaherty shook hands with Fordham, he handed over a map showing the layout of the base, the village and buildings in which all the soldiers were being held.

On 31 August, five of the eleven hostages were released. Kallay was given a satellite phone for easier contact, along with medical supplies in exchange for their release. The Royal Signals used this phone to get an exact location of the base at which the soldiers were being held. The West Side Boys used the satellite phone to contact the BBC and offered up a lengthy interview outlining their demands.

The West Side Boys seemed to have become increasingly, more and more frustrated with the negotiations and their behaviour became more erratic. This was due to the fact that many of them were high on cannabis and cocaine, making it an increasingly difficult and volatile situation to deal with. Their demands now consisted of immunity from prosecution, safe passage to the UK to take up university courses, and guaranteed acceptance to the reformed Sierra Leone Army.

Behind the scenes, a military operation was already being planned with the code name, 'Operation Barras.' This operation had to be planned and agreed on both a military and political level. Agreement now needed to be sought from the Sierra Leone government and even the local police force to hand over jurisdiction for the operation. During meetings with the West Side Boys, an SAS officer who was disguised as an Irish officer came to make notes about the area. It was soon discovered that due to the number of West Side Boys and the fact that there were two distinct locations (the village and their base), a much larger force would be required to execute the rescue mission, as opposed to just a Special Forces team. This led to 1 PARA, A Company being brought in for a combined operation. Attached to A Company were several specialist units from 1 PARA, including mortar, sniper, signals and a heavy machine gun section. On 31 August, A Company began its training under secrecy at South Cerney in Gloucestershire. On 5 September, the SAS was taken by SBS manned boats to observation posts just outside the West Side Boys' main camp. On approach from the river, the SAS and SBS realised that a water landing would be impossible due to the presence of high sandbanks and strong river flows.

The SAS set to work gathering information on weapons, size and the capability of the West Side Boys. They also looked for viable helicopter landing sites after it was deemed impossible to do an overland approach in vehicles due to road blocks and the fear that they would alert the enemy to their presence before they had had time to secure the hostages. In the end, the only insertion method available to them was by helicopter, so three Chinooks would carry all the personnel and drop them off at various landing sites. The SAS would use the fast rope technique and repel straight into the West Side Boys' base. The fast rope technique had first been used in combat during the Falklands War. The Paras were tasked with securing the village and providing fire support. By 9 September, negotiations had all but broken down after an unrealistic demand was made that a new government be put in place if the remaining soldiers were to be released. The SAS observation teams had also reported not having seen any of the captured soldiers for four days. This lead to the decision to begin Operation Barras the next day, and final approval was gained from Tony Blair and the Sierra Leonean President Ahmad Kabbah.

At 0615 hours the next morning, the three Chinooks, complete with two Lynx helicopters, took off and made their 15-minute journey to their holding point just out of sight and earshot of the West Side Boys. This hold was allowed to give the SAS teams at the observation posts time to move up onto the objective and secure the hostages the minute the attack started. The Chinooks made their final approach, flying in so low they blew off the tin roofs of several buildings, including the building that was guarding the soldiers. While the Chinooks dropped off the various teams, the two Lynx attack helicopters strafed various more heavily-armed positions around the base and the village. By the time the Chinooks had made it to their dropping-off period, the Lynx helicopters had made several successful passes, taking out enemy positions.

As the Chinooks were approaching, the SAS team from the observation post were already taking out any West Side Boys in the vicinity of the buildings in which the soldiers were being held. Many of the West Side Boys were still in bed, hung over from the night before, so their response to the attack was initially slow. The sound of C8s being fired from the SAS reverberated off the walls of the buildings, and the equally distinctive sound of AK-47s could be heard firing back. The Chinooks were now overhead and the rest of the SAS assault team fast-roped into position. It was during this time that the one and only fatal casualty of the operation occurred. Trooper Tinnion was shot in the chest and the exit wound was out via his shoulder. He was quickly pulled out and taken away for medical attention. Sadly, he died en route back to a medical facility.

The fire fight raged on in Gberi Bana. The West Side Boys fought back ferociously. Their fearlessness most likely came from the effects of drugs still in their system, either from the night before or from what they had taken when they awoke. The SAS moved forward and got all the hostages out safely. Less than 20 minutes since the SAS had begun, all the captured soldiers were on a helicopter. They looked physically and mentally shattered from their ordeal. The SAS continued to clear the area of Gberi Bana whilst 1 PARA was in its own intense fire fight at Magbeni.

The landing site for the Paras meant they had jumped off the ramp of the Chinook and into a swamp that was waist-deep, before making their way out. A small team of Paras had to stay in the swamp to ensure the LZ was kept secure. The various attachments got themselves ready and into position as the West Side Boys began to fire back. Rounds impacted on the bark of trees and sent splinters off in all directions. A heavy gun position was reported and quickly taken out by a Lynx helicopter. The Paras' mortar position opened up and began firing, although it was believed one mortar fell too close to the Paras, injuring seven, one of whom was Major Marshall, the company commander. This meant the 2iC had to take up command and keep the attack moving forward. As they got to the village, the Paras split up into teams, each one assaulting a different building. One at a time, they kicked the doors in and swept through. Once all the buildings had been cleared, the Paras set up defensive positions to ensure the village could not be retaken if a counter attack was mounted. At the same time, small patrols were sent into the surrounding jungle to flush out any West Side Boys hiding in the bushes and to ensure the whole area was secure. By 0800, the area was secure. 25 West Side Boys lay dead, and several more were captured. The number of dead may have been higher as bodies could have lain undiscovered in the jungle. It had been a fierce fight and the British had one dead and twelve wounded. The Paras remained in the area until 1400 hours. After the initial attack, they were tasked with destroying all the West Side Boys' vehicles and weapons, along with recovering the WMIKs which were attached to a Chinook and flown out of the area.

It had been a very successful mission and showed how well the Special Forces could work with other units. The success led to the Special Forces Support Group being set up and forming part of the Paras' structure. In the two weeks that followed, over 300 West Side Boys surrendered to the Jordanian peacekeeping force.

Operation Khukri

Operation Khukri was a multinational operation launched in the United Nations Assistance Mission in Sierra Leone (UNAMSIL), involving India, Britain, Nigeria and Ghana. The aim of the operation was to break the two-month long siege by the armed cadres of the Revolutionary United Front (RUF) around two companies of 5/8th Gorkha Rifles Infantry Battalion Group at Kailahun. By supporting a breakout and redeploying them with the main battalion at Daru.

The Indian 5/8th Gorkha Rifles, 14th Mechanised Infantry and elements of the 23rd Mechanised Infantry, together designated as INDBATT-1, had been sent to Sierra Leone to aid the Government in the disarmament of the RUF rebels. Two Rifle Companies had been kept as a QRF (Quick Reaction Force). Elements of the 9th Para, were also included. D squadron SAS were also present to guide in aviation units.

By mid-April 2000, two of the companies of INDBATT-1 were deployed in Kailahun, while the rest were deployed in Daru. On May 1, some elements of the RUF attacked and overran the KENBATT forces at Makeni. Due to a communication gap, the INDBATT-1 weren't informed, and some of their commanders at Kailahun, were captured the next day at a meeting with the RUF. Within ten days of this, the hostages were released due to intense pressure by INDBATT-1 and civilians.

The situation worsened and the RUF disarmed 500 Kenyan Peacekeepers, and began advancing towards Freetown. As panic broke out in Freetown, British troops evacuated the civilian staff at Freetown. The INDBATT-1 QRF was launched to Magburaka, where more Kenyans had been besieged. They made a 180 km advance, pushing back several ambushes, and rescuing the Kenyans. However, the situation at Kailahun kept deteriorating, and the 5/8th Gorkha Rifles were besieged and surrounded.

For 75 days the RUF rebels, had kept about 223 men of the 5/8th Gorkha Rifles under siege. As the situation worsened, the UN Force Commander, in consultation with the Sector Commander chose to use military action. The RUF rebels had six Brigades, one of which was deployed in the sector. It consisted of four main battalions, and one Strike Battalion. They were armed with AK-47s, RPGs, APCs, and SAMs. Each battalion was deployed in a particular area:

1st Battalion - Mobai

2nd Battalion - Kuiva

3rd Battalion - Neama

4th Battalion - Koindu

5th Battalion - Segbwema

The battle was planned to involve five phases:

Phase I: Mobilisation of UNAMSIL forces.

Phase II: Pre-emptive strikes by the helicopters, and breakout by the besieged forces at Kailahun. The UNAMSIL forces were to secure the area for a clear extraction.

Phase III: Link up of the besieged Kailahun column and Special Forces units at Giehun. 5/8 Gorkha Rifles (Daru column) to secure Pendembu.

Phase IV: Link up of Daru column and Kailahun column at Pendembu. Extraction to begin by air.

Phase V: All forces to fall back to Daru.

Phase I of the operation was the buildup of forces. Between 13th and 15th July 2000, the UNAMSIL forces were assembled at Daru and Kenewa. The IAF and RAF Aviation units were critical in the buildup, especially at Daru, since the area was cut off from the rest of the UN controlled areas. By midnight, 14 July, the buildup was complete.

The units at Kailahun were informed of the plan, and constantly kept in touch with the HQ through Satellite Phones. Since the operation required insertion by helicopters, the two companies at Kailahun were required to fall back 500 metres from the town itself, and secure two helipads for RAF Chinooks. By 0600 hours, 15 July, the Kailahun column had secured the helipads. Despite adverse weather conditions, two RAF Chinooks took off, and under guidance by SAS units dropped off the company from 2 Para, two kilometres south of Kailahun, landed at the helipads at 0620 hours, and extracted 33 personnel suffering from illness, as well as 11 Military Observers, before flying them back to Freetown. The plan involved the Indian MI-8s with greater firepower to aid in the assault, but they couldn't take-off due to adverse weather conditions.

Prior to the assault on the town, a barrage of rocket fire for ten minutes to suppress the enemy before the main offensive. Other fire came in the form of APCs, grenade launchers, mortars, and MMGs. The two INDBATT-1 companies at Kailahun began their assault at H hour to try and breakout of the town. The troops of Mechanised Company-1 of the besieged forces, were tasked to attack and capture the Kailahun Town Square. Motorised Rifle Company-1, was tasked with the capture the RUF checkpoint on the Daru-Kailahun Road. Mot-1 Company's advance was led by one platoon of the Ghatak (SF) Force, assisted by three BRDMs. Though the advance drew fire from nearby positions, the opposition was quickly neutralised by the BRDMs.

Mech-1 Company assaulted and captured the Town Square. Using it as a FUP, Mech-1 and Mot-1 Companies assaulted the checkpost on the road. The barrier at the checkpost was heavily defended, but after a fierce assault, the troops of Mot-1 Company fought through and captured the checkpost before securing the area. At 0730 hours, B-Vehicle column moved out with units from the 5/8th Gorkha Rifle Companies from Daru, and the NIBATT forces took their place at Daru. At the same time QRC was airlifted by MI-8s and dropped off at Area 3 to secure the bridges.

At 0738 hours 2 Para linked up with Mot-1 Company at the barrier, and began to advance to Giehun. The fire base at the Town Square remained in place until all the units had disengaged by fire and move. Mot-1 Company advanced quickly, while 2nd Para served as a rearguard, and took care of snipers along the way to Giehun. The RUF Forces reorganised and were constantly sniping down the rearguard, making the advance difficult and slow. At 0930 hours, Indian MI-35s arrived on the scene and provided fire support to the advancing columns, making their advance much swifter. At 0945 hours, one company 18th Grenadiers, part of the INDBATT-2, were airlifted and dropped off northeast of Giehun, where they awaited the arrival of the Kailahun column. By 1030 hours, the Kailahun column arrived at Giehun, where the Force Commander had been landed earlier. 60 of these troops were taken by helicopter to Daru.

After the airlift, the column reorganised and advanced towards Pendembu. They were faced with two major roadblocks along the road, the first was an eight feet ditch, and the second, a four feet deep one, each covered by troops with small arms and RPGs. Continuous sniping, and slushy roads hampered the progress, but the column secured the area, and using bridging stores carried in the column and dropped by the MI-8s, the units crossed the bridges, and continued on their way.

At 0620 hours, after the extraction of personnel at Kailahun, the INDBATT-2, INDMECH QRC, and the rest of the 5/8th Gorkha Rifles (Mot-2 Company) at Daru, commenced their operations. The 18th Grenadiers, alongside Infantry Fighting Vehicles from the Mech-2, and aided by artillery bombardment, secured a firm base along the road. Immediately after securing the base, the Daru Column advanced along the road, with Mech-2 Company's IFVs leading the advance. At 0830 hours, the column came under heavy fire from the north of the road, 500 metres short of Tikono. The IFVs neutralised the enemy and continued. The unit faced heavy resistance at both Bewobu, and Kuiva, but broke through with ease. Though the plan originally called for a physical capture and search of Kuiva, the speed of the advance of the Kailahun column, indicated a possibility of a linkup and evacuation on the same day. So the Daru Column continued to advance quickly to Pendembu. Though the rebels had dug-in positions in the town, they fled in the face of small arms fire by the column, and supporting fire from nearby mortars.

The column continued to move towards Area-3 bridges, suppressing enemy fire with their IFVs, while 9th Para, part of the battalion's QRC, was airlifted from Daru in 3 MI-8s, and secured the bridges in Area 3. Maintaining momentum, the column met up with the QRC forces near the bridges at 1230 hours, and continued onwards to Pendembu.

The Daru column and the QRC reached Pendembu, and prepared to assault the town. It was the HQ of the RUF 1st Brigade, and heavily defended. At 1300 hours, an attack helicopter made five passes over the town strafing the defenders, and performed pinpoint engaging of the defenders in their entrenched positions. Meanwhile, the mortars relocated to a location north of the Area 3 bridges. Mot-2 Company was to attack and secure the nearly 300 houses of the town, as well as an air head to the south-west. Mech-2 moved in from the north, and neutralised all the targets, and occupied the northern side of the town. Mot-2 moved up and silenced the enemy positions in the south-west corner, using the IFVs, and cleared the houses systematically with its riflemen. 4th Platoon of Mot-2, killed several rebels in the south-west pocket, and several more were killed in the armoury, cleared by 6th Platoon. A suitable airhead was established along the Daru-Pendembu road. All units linked up in the south-west corner, and reorganised into defensive positions for the evening.

At about 1630 hours, the IFV units advanced through the jungle to link up with Kailahun column. A link up was established at 1730 hours, and the entire force was gathered back at Pendembu by 1900 hours. The units took up defensive positions around and inside Pendembu. Any attempts by the RUF to counter-attack were thwarted with accurate fire from the troops. The routes used by the RUF for reinforcements were constantly shelled by mortars and a 105 mm Light Field Gun throughout the night.

On the 16 July 2000, at 0700 hours, Mot-2 prepared a helipad and readjusted the defences to prepare for the forthcoming helicopter extraction. At 0815 hours, MI-8s began arriving to extract the units. In 12 sorties, Mech-1 Company, Mot-1 Company, SF Company, D Company of 18 Grenadiers, and 2 Platoons of QRC Company were extracted. At 0930 hours, 50-60 enemies were spotted to the north of the town and effectively neutralised by the attack helicopters. The last MI-8s took off at 1030 hours. The battalion engineers demolished the selected RUF Bunkers, and the RUF ammunition store.

After the last helicopter took off, the remaining troops, consisting of Daru Column of 5/8th Gorkha Rifles, D-Company of 18th Grenadiers, remaining QRC Companies, and the vehicles of the Kailahun Companies, began to make their way back to Daru, with Mot-2 in the lead. Mech-2 was to hold on to the northern edge of town, and bring up the rear of the column, after a tactical disengagement. The column was constantly supported by one MI-35 helicopter at all times. After neutralising enemy positions at various bridges, the column reached Kuiva without incident. At Kuiva, the IFVs blind fired on any suspected enemy positions repeatedly to ensure the safety of the column.

Based on information from radio intercepts and intel, the columns were warned of an impending ambush cum roadblock near Kuiva. At 1400 hours, scout helicopters reported that the road between Kuiva and Bewabu had been dug up. The 18th Grenadiers secured the roadblock position, but the column had to be halted as they had stretched over too long a distance. At this time, one of the vehicles was attacked by an RPG. The riflemen and IFVs cleared the ambushing forces, and the column continued to advance.

At 1430 hours, near Bewabu, the leading IFVs came across a ditch, covered by heavy small arms fire from higher ground on both sides. The Commanding Officer realised that his troops were in the kill zone. He immediately sent 4 Rifle Platoon to engage the enemy targets. The firefight continued for fifteen minutes, and the MI-35 strafed enemies on both sides of the road. 6 Platoon and INDENG units bridged the gap, and the column immediately set off.

While the 5/8th Gorkha Rifles engaged the enemy at Bewabu, the 18th Grenadiers about six kilometres behind, supported by 2 BMPs from Mech-2, and 2 BRDMs of Mech-1, were engaged by enemy units just short of Kuiva. The units fought the enemy for about ten minutes, and continued to advance. About 500 metres from here, a vehicle carrying ammunition was hit by an RPG. The casualty was evacuated by a Chetak.

The convoy continued the rest of the way uneventfully. By 1730 hours, all the units had safely reached Daru. The operation was a complete success. All the besieged forces were evacuated successfully, with no UNAMSIL deaths. The units easily dealt with a handful ambushes sprung by the RUF on the way back

Operation Khukri was not a success simply in tactical terms. It was the worst defeat that the RUF has suffered in recent times, and was a tremendous boost to UNAMSIL morale. The Indian Forces were met with a rapturous welcome, as they marched triumphantly into Daru. The people of Sierra Leone helped build the Khukri War Memorial on the bank of the River Moa.

Operation Trent

The war in Afghanistan was brought about by the intervention in the Afghan Civil War by the United States. Following the terrorist attacks of September 11, 2001, the United States knew it needed to dismantle Al-Qaeda, an Islamic terrorist organization led by Osama bin Laden. The United States also wanted to capture Osma bin Laden, who was believed to be in Afghanistan. Another priority was the removal of the Taliban regime that in 2001 controlled around 90% of Afghanistan. The US President at the time, George W. Bush, demanded that the Taliban hand over Osama bin Laden and the Al-Qaeda leadership, which was supporting the Taliban in its war with the Northern Alliance. The Taliban took limited action by recommending that Osama bin Laden leaves the country, but refusing to extradite him without firm evidence from the United States that he had been involved in the 9/11 attacks. On this point the United States refused to negotiate. They planned and subsequently launched Operation Enduring Freedom on 7 October 2001 with the United Kingdom. They were later joined by other nations, including Canada, Australia, France and other mainly western allies, to attack the Taliban and Al-Qaeda forces in conjunction with the Northern Alliance.

During the initial phase of the war in Afghanistan, a small force of SAS and SBS were to see action in the country's deserts and mountains. The SBS would soon get themselves in one of the bloodiest and most controversial operations when they assisted in quashing a Taliban uprising at the Qala-i-janghi prison. The SAS had two full squadrons, A and G, in Afghanistan and had been deployed as part of Operation DETERMINE, which was a reconnaissance and bomb damage assessment mission. It was not the most exciting of operations for the SAS soldiers and at the time, America seemed wary of committing any ground troops, preferring to rely on air power and co-ordinate with Northern Alliance troops. Towards the end of November 2001, the SAS was given orders to attack a large opium storage facility that was also an Al-Qaeda base. It was located close to the southern border with Pakistan. Some 60-100 fanatical Al-Qaeda fighters occupied the heavily fortified base. At the time, the Americans regarded it as a low priority target; their first priority was to capture Osama bin Laden. The Americans were happy to destroy it from the air, but the British thought this may wipe out vital intelligence. The only way to capture this intelligence was with boots on the ground.

So that the SAS could co-ordinate their attack with American airstrikes, their assault was planned for mid-morning. It would be a frontal assault in broad daylight on an elevated position, without any real intelligence on the overall strength and positions of the enemy. Time was of the essence and a quick plan needed to be put in place. The plan would see Air Troop do a HALO (High Altitude Low Opening) parachute jump into the desert to secure an LZ for the six C-130 aircraft to land, bringing in A and G squadron members. This would give an assault force of over 120 men and 36 vehicles, mainly WIMIKs, along with ACMAT trucks and some scout motorcycles. The SAS soldiers would use the vehicles to drive to their designated FUP (Forming-Up Point). G Squadron was tasked with setting up a fire support base by 1100 hours and engaging enemy positions from a standoff point. American aircraft would destroy the opium storage.

Making use of the airstrike's and fire support from G Squadron, A Squadron would assault the opium base and do a sweep for any useful intelligence. The night before the C-130s were due to land, Air Troop performed their first operational HALO jump consisting of an eight-man team jumping off the ramp of a C-130. Once landed, Air Troop studied the ground to make sure it could carry the weight of a C-130 before they marked out a landing strip. As the C-130s came into land in the dark, Air Troop used infra-red torches to denote the landing zone

As the C-130s rolled to a stop, enveloped in the cloud of dust whipped up by their four large propellers, the rear ramp lowered and the WMIKs sped out and into an all-round defensive position. 30 minutes later, the C-130s had taken off to collect the rest of the SAS force. Once the entire force was at the LZ, the ACMAT trucks were piled high with supplies including fuel, water and ammo. The motorbikes went off first to scout for any enemy positions, as well as checking the routes the rest of the SAS convoy would travel. Under the cover of darkness, the largest wartime SAS force moved off to its LUP (Laying-Up Position) before moving out to commence the attack. The drive was thankfully uneventful, although one WMIK was lost after engine failure and abandoned where it had failed.

From the LUP, the force would move into their various FUPs before commencing the attack, although as they moved up towards the small group of buildings at the bottom of the mountainside, which was their objective, the Al-Qaeda defenders spotted the dust clouds being kicked up by their vehicles and started firing off RPGs with little success. The WMIKs lined up and started to rain down heavy fire from their 12.7 mm heavy machine guns and 7.62 mm GPMG.

A Squadron began to push forward, driving as close as possible before jumping off the WMIKs and moving forward. They used a technique called 'pepper potting,' which is one of the basic infantry manoeuvres taught to all British army recruits. The movement consists of a soldier getting up and moving forward whilst another is in the prone position giving covering fire, before the soldier moving forward goes firm. The soldier giving covering fire, gets up and moves past the soldier who has just gone firm and so on. In this case A Squadron moved up, with two giving covering fire whist two pushed forward.

The fire coming from Al-Qaeda was quite intense and whilst not very accurate, Al-Qaeda was fierce and almost seemed to be enjoying the fire fight. The fire support continued to rain down and snipers were also now in a position, armed with L82A1 Barret rifles, and took pot shots at various Al-Qaeda fighters. The snipers accounted for many of the Al-Qaeda fighters killed. While all this was going on, US Navy F/A18 Hornets were on station and began to fire Maverick missiles on the opium storage containers. The missiles destroyed some £50,000,000 ($78,520,000) worth of stored opium. The F/A18s also strafed various enemy positions that were pinning down the advancing SAS, narrowly missing the advancing SAS soldiers on one strafing run, which could have led to a blue-on-blue incident.

The SAS made slow but sure progress as every inch was a hard-fought one, such was the strength of the response from the Al-Qaeda fighters. As A Squadron got closer to the objective, they started to take casualties, one of which was serious. Rounds were dancing round their feet and ricocheting off the rocks around them. A Squadron finally made it to the main base and made their way through, clearing buildings and checking the HQ building for any useful intelligence. The battle had raged for four hours and the base was now littered with Al-Qaeda corpses.

The Regiment had taken relatively light casualties. Even though the base appeared clear, the SAS still need to undertake a tactical withdrawal just in case they came under renewed effective enemy fire. The four SAS casualties were evacuated by a US Chinook and the rest of the SAS returned to their LZ to be recovered by the same C-130s that had dropped them off.

Battle of Tora Bora

The hunt for Al-Qaeda was continuing in earnest in Afghanistan, Tora Bora was reported to be a large base; intelligence had it as an enormous fortress. The media made it out to be an impregnable cave fortress housing 2000 men complete with a hospital, a hydroelectric power plant, offices, a hotel, arms and ammunition stores, roads large enough to drive a tank into, and elaborate tunnel and ventilation systems. The actuality was very different - the Battle of Tora Bora ran from 12 December 2001 to 17 December 2001. It was believed that Osma bin Laden was hiding out in Tora Bora and there was also a large arms cash. This included deadly stinger missiles that had the Americans had supplied during the war against the Russians. Stinger missiles are highly accurate ground to air missiles and would pose a real threat against allied aircraft. An attack on Tora Bora was given high priority during the early stages of the Afghan War.

Tora Bora itself is a cave complex situated in the White Mountains of eastern Afghanistan, near the Khyber Pass. The Pashto meaning of Tora Bora is "black dust" or "black widow". During the early 1980's CIA agents had actually assisted the mujahedin in shoring up and extending the caves. This was for the Mujahedeen to hide out during the Soviet occupation. They were idea hideouts and staging posts to use to mount attacks from and store weapons and supplies in. Many of the caves have been used for centuries, as defensive positions during various wars and battles in Afghanistan. A British journalist Abdel had met Osma bin laden at Tora Bora in 1996 and his words were that Osma was living in a "humble cave with basic heating equipment."

On 3 December 2001 a group of CIA and Special Forces with the Codename 'Jawbreaker' was dropped into Jalalabad, Afghanistan by helicopter to begin an operation against Al-Qaeda in the Tora Bora region. The Northern Alliance managed to gain control of the low ground below the mountains were the Al-Qaeda fighters were holed up. The Jawbreaker team called in airstrikes and these airstrikes pushed al-Qaeda further up the mountains into more defensive and fortified positions. A week later 70 Delta Force operatives turned up, these were supplemented with SAS and U. S. Navy SEALs.

The Special Forces were used to mark out targets for the airstrikes which became deadly accurate. Many of the bombs hitting the exactly the same spot twice - forcing al-Qaeda fighters further into the caves to seek shelter. The area had the largest concentration of al-Qaeda fighters of the war, and they endured relentless pounding by American aircraft, as many as 100 airstrikes a day. One 15,000-pound bomb known as the 'Daisy Cutter' or 'BLU-82' was dropped from the rear of a C130. The BLU-82 was used up until 2008 when it was replaced with the GBU-43/B MOAB (Massive Ordnance Air Blast bomb).

al-Qaeda facing defeat, they decided to negotiate a truce with a local Commander of Afghan Militia. The truce was later believed to be a diversion to allow important individuals including Osman bin Laden to escape. On 12 December the fighting flared up again, possibly to buy time for the main force to escape via the White Mountains into Pakistan. Special Forces along with Tribal forces and continued air support pushed forward towards the fortified Al-Qaeda positions that were scattered in caves and bunkers across the region. Twelve SBS accompanied Delta Force on the attack against the Tora Bora cave complex. Special Force operators from the German KSK Kommando Spezialkräfte also took part in the battle. They were given the task of protecting the flanks in the mountains and had also conducted reconnaissance missions. Local tribal Militia started to amass and these were paid for by the U.S. They made up a force of around 2000 and were waiting to move forward once the heavy bombing had ceased and weakened al-Qaeda positions. Even though the bombing had weakened positions the cave complex itself still required cave by cave clearance and it involved quite an intense firefight the flush out the final al-Qaeda fighters. Many al-Qaeda fighters had fled over the rough terrain into Pakistan as the battle entered its final stages. Over 200 al-Qaeda fighters had been killed and the cave complex at Tora Bora had been captured. The cave complex turned out to be nothing like it had been made out to be in the media.

After the successful Battle of Tora Bora, al-Qaeda forces simply went into hiding rather than giving up. An interim Afghan government was set up in Kabul. At the same time anti U.S forces were also being built up and were operating against the Americans during Operation Anaconda. U.S. forces set up their main base at Bagram after the SBS had helped seize it.

An American report released on 30 November 2009 titled, 'Tora Bora Revisited: How we failed to get bin Laden and why it matters today.' The report outlined the failings and the fact that by not completing the job in 2001 the war in Afghanistan had become more protracted. It had made it harder to make the country more stable.

"Removing the al-Qaeda leader from the battlefield eight years ago would not have eliminated the worldwide extremist threat. But the decisions that opened the door for his escape to Pakistan allowed Osman bin Laden to emerge as a potent symbolic figure who continues to attract a steady flow of money and inspire fanatics worldwide."

Battle for Qala-i-Janghi

Afghanistan has seen the SBS utilised like never before, even on land-based missions where their skill and expertise is just as valuable as those of the SAS. From the start of Operation Enduring Freedom in Afghanistan, the SBS were given important tasks such as securing Bagram airbase and one of the bloodiest battles of the war in Afghanistan. In November 2001, the campaign against the Taliban was in full swing and had captured over 600 Taliban and al-Qaeda prisoners. On 24 November 2001, foreign Taliban suspects were transported to the fortress, which had now been turned into a prison. The prisoners had not been searched, and some had concealed weapons during the surrender. On the day of the surrender, prisoners with grenades had committed suicide and killed two of Dostum's commanders in separate incidents at the makeshift prison. Despite the four deaths, the allies did not reinforce security at the prison.

Nearly all of these prisoners were being held in a large fort complex called Qala-i-Janghi, near Mazar-i-Sharif, which was in the north of Afghanistan. At the time, many of the prisoners were in the courtyard of the fort being interrogated by two CIA agents. All of a sudden, the prisoners, for some unknown reason, decided to revolt and killed one of the agents. The other agent fled for his life into the fort. The prisoners stormed the fort and raided the armoury, taking AK-47s and RPGs. The small group of US and Northern Alliance soldiers guarding the fort were going to be overwhelmed by this now armed uprising. A nine-man US Special Forces team and an eight-man SBS patrol were in the area and had been tasked as a QRF for the region. They responded immediately to the call for assistance and drove quickly to the fort, arriving at 1400 hours. By the time they got there, the battle was already in full swing. The prisoners were almost on the verge of breaking out of the fort. The SBS team lined up around the fort's battlements and began to engage the prisoners. The SBS came under heavy fire from the prisoners, who had become very organised and determined to get out of the prison. The SBS decided to dismount their GPMGs from their WMIKs and carried them to the battlements to place more direct fire each time the prisoners tried to push forward and overrun the defending forces. From 4pm until nightfall, nine airstrikes were directed against the entrenched prisoners, who continued to put up a fierce resistance. Despite requests, the US aircraft dropped several 500-pound precision-guided bombs to try to destroy the armoury, which was serving as a firebase for the prisoners. While all this was going on, the SBS started to plan the rescue of the second CIA agent, who had not been heard from. This team of SBS soldiers braved intense enemy fire and minefields to reach the building where the agent was sheltering. The rescue mission was fraught with danger and the odds were stacked against them. However, they managed to fight their way to the fort. What the SBS had not realised was that the CIA agent had already managed to escape and was being debriefed at the HQ in Mazar. That night, two AC-130 Spectre gunships circled over the fort and fired thousands of rounds at the prisoners. During the intense fire that was poured onto the prisoners, the ammunition depot was hit, creating a huge explosion which continued to burn throughout the night. By the next day resistance had slackened and the Northern Alliance, supported by tanks and APCs, mounted an attack and by the end of the day had re-captured most of the fort. The body of the CIA agent who had been killed was recovered, although he had been booby trapped with a grenade. At the centre of the fort there was a series of tunnels and a holding cell containing prisoners who refused to surrender. Northern Alliance soldiers fired into the cell and also threw grenades, with little effect. They poured in oil and set it alight. This also failed to dislodge the prisoners and on 28 November, General Dostum arrived to try and get the rest of the prisoners to surrender, but to no avail.

On 29 November, he ordered the cell to be flooded using very cold water from the irrigation system, and this led to the final surrender of the prisoners on 1th December. Out of the original 300-500 prisoners thought to be at the fort, only 86 had survived. Some of the prisoners after the battle were found to have had their gold fillings removed as Northern Alliance soldiers had looted them and killed two wounded prisoners. Some of the dead prisoners were found with their hands tied behind their backs. Due to the high number of prisoner casualties and the use of heavy weaponry against them, the Northern Alliance and the coalition were accused of breaking the Geneva Conventions by using disproportionate means on the prisoners, even though the prisoners had been heavily armed themselves with AK-47s, RPGs and Mortars.

Theatre Siege Moscow - Spetsnaz

On 23 October 2002, the Moscow theatre Dubrovka in Moscow was seized by 40 to 50 armed Chechens who claimed allegiance to the Islamist militant separatist movement in Chechnya. The hostage crisis, also known as the 2002 Nord-Ost siege, The group took 850 hostages and demanded the withdrawal of Russian forces from Chechnya along with an end to the Second Chechen War. The siege was officially led by Movsar Barayev aged 23 the nephew of a Chechen rebel militia commander Arbi Barayev who had died in battle.

The raid was undertaken by Spetznaz meaning "special purpose", is a general term used for a variety of special operations forces or regular forces assigned to special tasks. You can trace the inception of Spetznaz back to 1938. However, during World War II, the Red Army reconnaissance and sabotage detachments were formed under the supervision of the Second Department of the General Staff of the Soviet Armed Forces. These forces were subordinate to front commanders. The infamous NKVD internal security and espionage agency also had their own special purpose (osnaz) detachments, including many saboteur teams who were airdropped into enemy-occupied territories to work with and more normally take over the Soviet Partisans.

In 1950, Georgy Zhukov advocated the creation of 46 military Spetsnaz companies, each consisting of 120 servicemen. This was the first use of "Spetsnaz" to denote a separate military branch since World War II. These companies were later expanded to battalions and onto brigades. However, some separate companies (orSpN) and detachments (ooSpN) existed with brigades until the dissolution of the Soviet Union.

The hostages in the Dubrovka theatre were seized 23 October 2003 at the House of Culture of State Ball-Bearing Plant Number 1 in the Dubrovka area of Moscow about 4km southeast of the Kremlin. During Act II of a sold-out performance of Nord-Ost a little after 2100 hours, 40–50 heavily armed and masked men and women dressed in black camouflage drove in a bus to the theatre and entered the main hall firing assault rifles in the air. They took approximately 850–900 people hostage, including members of the audience and performers, among them an MVD general. The reaction of spectators inside the theatre to the news that the theatre was under terrorist attack was not uniform - some people remained calm, some reacted hysterically, and others fainted. Some performers who had been resting backstage escaped through an open window and called police; in all, some 90 people managed to flee the building or hide during the initial attack. Barayev told the hostages that the attackers, who identified themselves as a suicide squad from the 29th Division, had no grudge against foreign nationals and promised to release anyone who showed a foreign passport. In the theatre there were about 75 foreign nations, from 14 countries, including Australia, Germany, the Netherlands, Ukraine, the United Kingdom and the United States.

The hostage takers soon made their demands known that unless Russian forces were immediately and unconditionally withdrawn from Chechnya. They would begin to kill the hostages after the deadline, which was one week.

The media managed to get hold of a videotaped in which the gunmen declared their willingness to die for their cause. The statement in the video was as follows:

"Every nation has the right to their fate. Russia has taken away this right from the Chechens and today we want to reclaim these rights, which Allah has given us, in the same way he has given it to other nations. Allah has given us the right of freedom and the right to choose our destiny. And the Russian occupiers have flooded our land with our children's blood. And we have longed for a just solution. People are unaware of the innocent who are dying in Chechnya: the sheikhs, the women, the children and the weak ones. And therefore, we have chosen this approach. This approach is for the freedom of the Chechen people and there is no difference in where we die, and therefore we have decided to die here, in Moscow. And we will take with us the lives of hundreds of sinners. If we die, others will come and follow us—our brothers and sisters who are willing to sacrifice their lives, in Allah's way, to liberate their nation. Our nationalists have died, but people have said that they, the nationalists, are terrorists and criminals. But the truth is Russia is the true criminal."

Even if Russia had been prepared to meet the hostage takers' demands, a week was not long enough to withdraw all the troops from Chechnya.

The hostage-takers demanded termination of the use of artillery and air forces in Chechnya starting the next day. Russian forces ceased using heavy weapons until 28 September, a halt to the notorious mopping-up operations, and that President of Russia Vladimir Putin should publicly declare that he was striving to stop the war in Chechnya. By the time of the hostage-taking, the conflict in the embattled republic was killing an average of three federal troops daily.

Cell phone conversations between the hostages trapped in the building and their family members revealed that the hostage-takers had grenades, mines and IEDs strapped to their bodies. They had deployed more explosives throughout the theatre both a booby traps and to potentially destroy the building. The militants used Arabic names among themselves, and the female terrorists wore Arab-style burqa clothes which are highly unusual attire for the region they came from. However, Chechnya's Muslims had no information about who the attackers were and condemned attacks on civilians. The pro-Moscow Islamic leader of Chechnya also condemned the attack.

All hostages were being kept in the auditorium and the orchestra pit was used as a lavatory. The situation in the hall was nervous and it frequently changed depending on the mood of the hostage-takers, who were following reports in the mass media. The news could also send them into a spin threatening hostages or saying they would blow up the building. The information the media had and was broadcasting was not necessarily the whole picture or truth. The hostage takers let members of the audience make phone calls. One of the hostages used her mobile phone to plead with the authorities not to storm the auditorium, as truckloads of police and soldiers with armoured vehicles surrounded the building.

During the 23 October, the attackers released 150 to 200 people, including children, pregnant women, Muslims, some foreign-born theatre-goers and people requiring health treatment in the early hours after they invaded. Two women, managed to escape during the process of releasing some of the hostages. The terrorists then said they were ready to kill 10 hostages for any of their number killed if the security forces intervened.

At 0130 hours Olga Romano a 26-year-old Russian civilian described as 'strong-willed', and lived near the theatre. She entered the theatre, crossing the police cordon undetected by herself. Once inside the theatre, she began urging the hostages to stand up to their captors. This caused considerable confusion in the auditorium. The hostage takers believed she was a Federal Security Service (FSB) agent and was shot and killed several seconds later. Romanova's body was later removed from the building by a Russian medical team, incorrectly reported by the Moscow police as the body of the first hostage who was killed while trying to escape.

On day two of the siege, 24 October 2002, the Russian government offered the hostage-takers the opportunity to leave for any third country. The suborned hostages made an appeal, possibly under orders or duress, to Putin to cease hostilities in Chechnya and asked him to refrain from assaulting the building. Because of the crisis, Putin cancelled an overseas trip that would have included meetings with U.S. President George W. Bush and other world leaders. Well-known public and political figures such as Aslambek Aslakhanov, Irina Khakamada, Ruslan Khasbulatov, Joseph Kobzon, Boris Nemtsov and Grigory Yavlinsky took part in negotiations with the hostage-takers. Ex-President of the Soviet Union Mikhail Gorbachev also announced his willingness to act as an intermediary in the course of negotiations. The hostage takers also demanded that representatives of the International Red Cross and Médecins Sans Frontières come to the theatre to lead negotiations. FSB Colonel Konstantin Vasilyev attempted to enter the patio of the theatre, but was shot at while approaching the building and forced to retreat. During the 24 October, another 39 hostages were set free by the hostage takers. The ensure that one of the hostages reiterated to the authorities the threat of hostages being killed if their demands were not met. Negotiations on the release of non-Russian nationals were undertaken by various embassies and the Chechens promised to release all foreign hostages. The hostage takers claimed they were ready to release 50 Russian hostages if Akhmad Kadyrov, head of Chechnya's pro-Moscow administration, would come to the theatre, but Kadyrov did not respond, and the release did not take place.

During the night of the 23-24 October a water piped had burst, flooding the ground floor. However, the hostage takers saw this as a purposeful act on the part of the Russian authorities. The sewage system was being used by Russian special forces to 'listen in', so they may have inadvertently caused the pipe to burst.

During the 25 October, various individuals took took part in negotiations with the militants. Including journalists Anna Politkovskaya,

Sergei Govorukhin and Mark Franchetti, public figures Yevgeny Primakov, Ruslan Aushev and again Aslambek Aslakhanov. The hostages, however, wanted a representative of Vladamir Putin.

The hostage takers agreed to release 75 foreign citizens in the presence of diplomatic representatives of their states. 15 Russian citizens were released, including eight children. After a meeting with Putin, the FSB head Nikolai Patrushev offered to spare the lives of the Chechens if they released the remaining hostages unharmed.

A group of Russian doctors, including Dr. Leonid Roshal, head of the Medical Center for Catastrophes, entered the theatre to bring medicine for the hostages and said the hostage takers were not beating or threatening their captives. He also said that most of the hostages were calm, with only a couple of the hostages possibly three, who were hysterical. The Red Cross had also taken some hot food, warm clothes and medicine in.

An NTV channel journalist recorded an interview with Barayev, in which he sent a message to the Russian government:

"We have nothing to lose. We have already covered 2,000 kilometres by coming here. There is no way back... We have come to die. Our motto is freedom and paradise. We already have freedom as we've come to Moscow. Now we want to be in paradise."

During the interview Barayev also said that the group had come to Moscow not to kill the hostages or to fight with Russia's elite troops, as they had had enough fighting in Chechnya over the years, "We came here with a specific aim — to put an end to the war and that is it."

After dusk, on the 25 October a man identified as Gennady Vlakh ran across the square and gained entry to the theatre. He said that his son was among the hostages, but his son did not seem to be present and the man was led away and shot by the hostage takers, believing he was a spy. There is considerable confusion surrounding this incident, and Vlakh's body was cremated before it was identified.

Around midnight, a gunfire incident took place as Denis Gribkov, a 30-year-old male hostage, ran over the backs of theatre seats towards the female insurgents who were sitting next to a large IED. Another male hostage taker shot at him, but missed. However, stray bullets hit and severely wounded two other hostages who were evacuated from the building soon after. Gribkov was removed from the auditorium and later found dead from gunshot wounds.

During the night of the 25 October, Akhmed Zakayev, a Chechen envoy and associate of the separatist President Aslan Maskhadov, appealed to the extremists and asked them to "refrain from rash steps". The Chechens told the BBC that a special representative of President Putin planned to come to the theatre for talks the next day. Two members of the Spetznaz Alpha Group moving around in the no-man's land surrounding the theatre were seriously wounded by a grenade fired from the building by the terrorists, which was blamed by the Moscow police chief Vladimir Pronin on the media news leak.

In the early hours of 26 October 2002, forces from Russia's FSB (Alpha Group and Vympel), with the assistance of the Russian Ministry of Internal Affairs (MVD) SOBR unit, surrounded and stormed the theatre, first via the Central Station club that had opened a month prior in the underground level of the building. All the special forces were heavily armed and masked.

Deputy Interior Minister Vladimir Vasilyev stated that the raid was prompted by a panic among the captives due to the execution of two female hostages. The raid was planned shortly after the hostages were initially seized and the shooting had occurred about three hours before the operation began.

Early in the morning before dawn, at around 0500 hours, the searchlights that had been illuminating the main entrance to the theatre went out. Inside, although many hostages at first took the gas to be smoke from a fire, it soon became apparent to everyone that a mysterious gas had been pumped into the building. Different reports said it came either through the specially created hole in the wall or that it was pumped through the theatre ventilation system, or that it emerged from beneath the stage. It is thought that the security services pumped an aerosol anaesthetic, later conjectured to be weaponised fentanyl a potent, synthetic opioid analgesic with a rapid onset and short duration of action. The discovery of a gas attack caused panic in the auditorium. Hostage Anna Andrianova, a correspondent for Moskovskaya Pravda, called Echo of Moscow radio studio and told on-air in a live broadcast interview that the government forces had begun an operation by pumping gas into the hall.

"It seems to us that the Russians have started something. Please, give us a chance. If you can do anything, please do! ... I don't know which gas it is. But I see [the Chechens'] reactions. They don't want our deaths, and our officials want none of us to leave alive! I don't know. We see it, we feel it; we are breathing through our clothes. ... It began from outside. That's what our government has decided — that no one should leave from here alive. ...."

The hostage takers, some of whom were equipped with gas masks, responded by firing at the Russian positions outside. After around thirty minutes, when the gas had taken effect, a physical assault on the building commenced. The combined forces entered through numerous building openings, including the roof, the basement, and finally the front door. When the shooting began, the terrorists told their hostages to lean forward in the theatre seats and cover their heads behind the seats. Some of the hostages reported that some people in the audience fell asleep, and some of the hostage takers put on respirators. As the hostage takers and hostages began to fall unconscious, several of the female hostage takers made a dash for the balcony but passed out before they reached the stairs. They were later found shot dead. Two of the Alpha Group was also overcome by the gas.

After nearly one and a half hours of sporadic gun battles, the Russian Special Forces blew open the doors to the main hall and moved into the auditorium. In a fierce firefight, the federals killed most of the hostage takers, both those still awake and those who had succumbed to the gas.

According to the Russian government, the fighting between the troops and the still-conscious hostage takers continued in other parts of the building for another 30 minutes to one hour. Spetsnaz Alpha team troops said that "this is our first successful operation for years". At 0700 hours, rescuers began carrying the bodies of hostages out of the building. Bodies were laid in rows on the foyer and the pavement at the main entrance to the theatre, unprotected from falling rain and snow. None of the bodies witnessed by The Guardian correspondent had bullet wounds or showed signs of bleeding, "their faces were waxy, white and drawn, their eyes open and blank." Shortly, the entire space was filled with bodies and those unconscious from the gas but still alive.

Ambulances were standing by and ordinary city buses were brought in. Medical workers were expecting to treat victims of explosions and gunfire, but not a secret chemical agent. The drug naloxone counteracts the chemical agent's effects, but would have to have been administered by rescue workers immediately. Based on the gas's effects and examinations of victims later on, it appeared what was used, was to have been an FSB-made aerosol version of 3-methylfentanyl known as Kolokol-1, an artificial, powerful opium-like substance. However, Government officials still treat its contents as a state secret and why no doctors were informed of what it was and how the effects of the gas could be properly treated.

The bodies of dead hostages were put in two buses which were parked at the TC. Initial reports said nothing about casualties among the hostages. The crisis HQ representatives went to the college hall, where relatives of the hostages had been waiting, and told them that allegedly there were no fatalities among the hostages. The first official report of fatalities among the hostages came at about 0900 hours, despite the death of five children, which had been already reported by medical personnel, the official statement claimed there were no children among the dead.

At 1300 hours, Vasilyev announced at a press conference a death toll of 67 hostages, who he said were killed by the hostage takers, but again stated that no children or any foreigners were among those killed. Armed guards were posted at the hospitals where victims were taken and doctors were ordered not to release any of the theatre patients in case any hostage takers had concealed themselves among the hostages.

Panic started to set in amongst the families of the hostages, as information was being withheld by the government. Even information about those that had been hospitalised had been suppressed.

The official number of the dead rose to 90, including 25 children, while it was still claimed that the final attack was provoked by the terrorists executing their captives. Later the same day, the official death toll among hostages had risen to at least 118 and the officials had still not specified exactly what killed them. It seemed as if the government were trying to cover something up and operating in the old cold war Russia with being very clandestine. By 28 October, of the 646 former hostages who remained hospitalised, 150 were still in intensive care and 45 were in critical condition.

Seventy-three hostages, including six children, required no medical attention. There were several Chechens among the hostages and it may be that some of them were not treated because of their Chechen names. Money and other valuables belonging to the victims vanished; official reports stated that the valuables were stolen by an FSB officer who was later killed in a car crash. The Russian authorities initially maintained that none of the deaths among the hostages occurred through poisoning. The authorities made suggestions that pre-existing health conditions or health conditions brought on by the stress and very little food or water had caused many of the deaths.

The complete death toll ended up as all 40 of the hostage takers and about 130 hostages, which died during the raid or in the following days. Doctor Andrei Seltsovsky, Moscow's health committee chairman, announced that all but one of the hostages killed in the raid had died of the effects of the unknown gas rather than from gunshot wounds. The cause of death listed for all hostages was declared to be "terrorism", claiming they died from heart attacks or other physical ailments. Among the deaths, 17 were Nord-Ost cast members, including two child actors. Of the foreign nationals, three were from Ukraine, one was American, and the others were citizens of Austria, Armenia, Belarus, Kazakhstan and the Netherlands. About 700 surviving hostages were poisoned by gas, and some of them received injuries leading to disabilities from medium to severe. Most, if not all, of the hostage deaths, were caused by suffocation when hostages collapsed on chairs with heads falling back or were transported and left lying on their backs by rescue workers; in such a position, tongue prolapse causes blockage of breathing. Several Russian Special Forces operatives were also poisoned by the gas during the operation. The full death toll is still slightly disputed with some figures of around 200.

Responsibility for the act of terrorism was placed with the Chechen radical militant groups the Special Purpose Islamic Regiment (SPIR), the International Islamic Peacekeeping Brigade (IIPB) and the Riyadus-Salikhin Reconnaissance and Sabotage Battalion of Chechen Martyrs took part in the operation. In 2003, the United States designated the three groups as terrorist organizations, describing them as violent, responsible for numerous acts of terrorism with links to the al-Qaeda network. The same U.S. statement also reaffirmed their support for a political settlement to the Chechen conflict and urged Russia to pursue such a solution.

Shamil Basayev posted a statement on his website claiming ultimate responsibility for the incident, resigning all official positions within the Chechen government and promising new attacks. He also apologised to Chechnya's elected president and separatist leader Aslan Maskhadov for not informing him of the planned raid and asked him for forgiveness. Basayev defended the hostage-taking for giving "all Russians a first-hand insight into all the charms of the war unleashed by Russia and take it back to where it originated from" and said that his next "main goal will be destroying the enemy and exacting maximum damage" and "the next time, those who come won't make any demands, won't take hostages." A series of suicide bombings aimed at civilian targets in Russia followed in 2003 and 2004.

The Russian government claimed that wiretapped phone conversations prove that Maskhadov knew of the plans in advance, which he denied. Maskhadov and his representatives in the West condemned the attack which they said had nothing to do with official policy. Maskhadov said he felt responsible for those "who resorted to self-sacrifice in despair", but also said the "barbaric and inhumane policies" of the Russian leadership were ultimately to blame and criticized the storming of the theatre. He offered to start unconditional peace talks with the Russian government to find a political solution to the conflict in Chechnya.

The siege was seen as a public relations disaster for Maskhadov. Some commentators suggested that Movladi Udugov was in charge from behind the scenes. Russian military expert Pavel Felgenhauer suggested that the aim of the extremist leaders seemed to have been to provoke the Russian government forces "to kill ethnic Russians in Moscow on a large scale", which happened. According to the report by Russian investigators, Zura Barayeva, the widow of Arbi Barayev, led the female members of the group, while a man known as Yasir, identified by his documents as Idris Alkhazurov, was said to be the group's "ideologist" believed to be trained in Saudi Arabia. Russian officials said Chechen militants received financing from groups based in Turkey and that they intercepted telephone calls from the captors to unidentified embassies in Moscow, as well as to Turkey and unidentified Arab states.

After the raid, Moscow Mayor Yuri Luzhkov said that "the operation was carried out brilliantly by special forces"; he claimed he had wanted a negotiated end to the crisis, but the final attack was made necessary by the reported killing of hostages. The Russian presidential special envoy for human rights in Chechnya, Abdul-Khakim Sultygov, said the bloody outcome was "a good lesson to the terrorists and their accomplices."

Deputy Interior Minister Vasilyev launched a Moscow-wide operation to catch anyone who may have helped the militants, while his boss, Interior Minister Boris Gryzlov, urged people to be vigilant and to report anyone acting suspiciously to police. On 29 October, Vasilyev said he only had the authority to state that special chemical agents had been used and that some 30 suspected militants and their collaborators, including several civil servants and security officers, had been arrested around the theatre and in other parts of the city in what Gryzlov called an "unprecedented operation" to identify what he described as a vast terrorist network in Moscow and the surrounding region. Russian President Vladimir Putin defended the scale and violence of the assault in a televised address later on the morning of 26 October 2002, stating that the government had "achieved the near impossible, saving hundreds... of people" and that the rescue "proved it is impossible to bring Russia to its knees". Putin thanked the Special Forces as well as the Russian citizens for their "bravery" and the international community for the support given against the "common enemy". He also asked forgiveness for not being able to save more of the hostages, and declared Monday a national day of mourning for those who died. He vowed to continue fighting "international terrorism".

On 29 October 2002, Putin released another televised statement, saying: "Russia will respond with measures that are adequate to the threat to the Russian Federation, striking all the places where the terrorists themselves, the organizers of these crimes and their ideological and financial inspirations are. I stress, wherever they may be located." It was commonly assumed Putin was threatening the former Soviet Republic of Georgia. Putin's comments came as British Prime Minister Tony Blair phoned him to congratulate him on the ending of the siege. President Putin was unhappy with the coverage of the hostage crisis by NTV, the last nationwide TV channel effectively independent of the government.

In January 2003 the management of NTV was replaced, resulting in a profound effect on its editorial policy.

The attacks prompted Putin's government to tighten Russia's grip on Chechnya. On 28 October 2002, two days after the crisis, he announced that unspecified measures adequate to the threat would be taken in response to terrorist activity from this point forward. With reports of 30 fighters killed near the Chechen capital Grozny. The Russian Ministry of Defence cancelled plans to reduce the 80,000 troop presence in the tiny breakaway republic. In early November, Defence Minister Sergei Ivanov announced Russian troops had launched large-scale operations against separatists throughout Chechnya. The actions of the military caused a new wave of refugees, according to the pro-Moscow Chechen official and the hostage crisis negotiator Aslanbek Aslakhanov.

On 29 May 2008, the European Court of Human Rights (ECHR) unanimously condemned Russia for enforced disappearances in five cases from Chechnya, including the disappearance of two young women in Ulus-Kert the prosecutor's office initially stated to media that Aminat Dugayeva and Kurbika Zinabdiyeva had been arrested on suspicion of involvement with the Moscow siege.

President Maskhadov's unconditional offer for peace talks with Russia was dismissed, and Russian Foreign Minister Sergei Lavrov compared such calls with the suggestion that Europe should conduct such talks with the former al-Qaeda leader Osama bin Laden. Russia also accused Akhmed Zakayev of involvement in the attack. When he visited Denmark for a peace congress in October 2002, the World Chechen Congress event in Copenhagen. The Russians demanded his arrest and extradition - Zakayev was held for over a month, but was released after Danish authorities stated they were not convinced that sufficient evidence had been provided. The Kremlin also accused the Danish authorities of siding with the Chechens by allowing the meeting of about 100 Chechens, Russian human rights activists and lawmakers from Russia and other European countries to gather and discuss ways to end the fighting.

In 2003, Human Rights Watch reported Chechens in Moscow were subjected to increased police harassment after the hostage crisis. Moscow's Chechens rose in numbers from about 20,000 in the Soviet period to an estimated 80,000 in 2002. Many in the Russian press and in the international media warned that the death of so many hostages in the Special Forces' rescue operation would severely damage President Putin's popularity. Shortly after the siege, the Russian president had record public approval ratings; in December 2002, 83% of Russians reportedly declared themselves satisfied with Putin's rule and his handling of the siege.

The official investigation that the Moscow City Prosecutor's Office took over three and a half years, but failed to provide positive information on the gas agent that killed hostages, possible antidote to that agent, the number of hostages released by the operation, the number of hostage takers who had seized the theatre, Russian authorities had reported 40, but hostages thought there were 50. The names of officials who had made the decision about the assault ere also omitted from the report. On 1 June 2007, news came that the official investigation had been suspended. The reason provided was that the "culprit had not been located".

The same month, Tatiana Karpova, co-chair of the Nord-Ost Organization of former hostages and the families of the dead, demanded a new criminal investigation. She claimed the authorities failed to meet their obligations related to the care of the hostages before and after the operation. She stated her concern about the lack of medical care for the injured, and future medical problems for the survivors.

An independent investigation of the event was undertaken by Russian politicians Sergei Yushenkov, Sergei Kovalev, journalist Anna Politkovskaya, Hoover Institute scholar John B. Dunlop, and former FSB officers Aleksander Litvinenko and Mikhail Trepashkin. According to their version, FSB knew about the terrorist group's arrival in Moscow and directed them to the theatre through their agent provocateur Khanpasha Terkibayev ("Abu Bakar"), whose name was in the list of hostage takers and who left the theatre alive. In April 2003 Litvinenko gave information about Terkibayev to Sergei Yushenkov when he visited London. Yushenkov passed this file to Politkovskaya and she was able to interview Terkibayev in person. A few days later, Yushenkov was assassinated by gunfire in Moscow. Terkibayev was later killed in an apparent car crash in Chechnya.

After the siege, 61 former hostages started seeking compensation for physical and emotional suffering totaling almost $60m from Moscow city authorities. According to Russia's-new anti-terrorism law, the region where an act of terror occurs should pay compensation for moral and material damages. Moscow mayor Yuri Luzhkov's office denounced the suits, saying it could not be held responsible as "the Chechen issue and its consequences are not within the jurisdiction of the Moscow authorities in any way." The Moscow administration earlier agreed to pay 50,000 roubles ($1,570) in compensation to each former hostage and 100,000 roubles ($3,140) to relatives of those killed. In all but one of the cases, Moscow city courts rejected the compensation claims.

On 20 December 2011, the European Court of Human Rights published its judgement in the case, ordering Russia to pay the 64 applicants a total of 1.3 million euros in compensation. The court also found that Russia had violated Article 2 of the European Convention on Human Rights when handling the hostage crisis, "with inadequate planning and conduct of the rescue operation", and with the "authorities' failure to conduct an effective investigation into the rescue operation", although the Court found that there had been "no violation of Article 2 of the Convention on account of the decision by the authorities to resolve the hostage crisis by force and to use the gas."

Since the end of the Second Chechen War in May 2000, low-level insurgency has continued, particularly in Chechnya, Ingushetia and Dagestan. Russian security forces have succeeded in capturing some of their leaders, such as Shamil Basayev, who was killed on July 10, 2006. Since Basayev's death, Dokka Umarov has taken the leadership of the rebel forces in North Caucasus.

Radical Islamists from Chechnya and other North Caucasian republics have been held responsible for a number of terrorist attacks throughout Russia, most notably the Russian apartment bombings in 1999, the Moscow theatre hostage crisis in 2002 described above, the Beslan school hostage crisis in 2004, the 2010 Moscow Metro bombing and the Domodedovo International Airport bombing in 2011.

Beslan school hostage crisis

On the 1 September 2004 the Beslem School was seized by a group of armed Islamic separatist militants, mostly Ingush and Chechen. The Beslem School was in the town of Beslan, North Ossetia in the North Caucasus region of the Russian Federation. The hostage-takers were the Riyadus-Salikhin Battalion. They had been sent by the Chechen separatist warlord Shamil Basayev, who demanded recognition of the independence of Chechnya and the Russian withdrawal from Chechnya. The event led to security and political repercussions in Russia; most notably it contributed to a series of federal government reforms consolidating power in the Kremlin and strengthening of the powers of the President of Russia.

The school was one of seven schools in Beslan, a town of around 35,000 people. The school, located next to the district police station, with around 60 teachers and more than 800 students.

On 1 September 2004, which was the traditional start of the Russian school year. It was an important day, where the children, accompanied by their parents and other relatives, attend ceremonies hosted by their school. Due to the Knowledge Day festivities, the number of people in the schools was higher than there would be on a normal school day with parents attending. Early in the morning, a group of twenty-four heavily armed Islamic-nationalists left a forest encampment located in the vicinity of the village of Psedakh in the neighbouring republic of Ingushetia, east of North Ossetia and west of war-torn Chechnya. These soon to be hostage takers, wore green military camouflage and black balaclava masks. Some of them were also wearing explosive belts and explosive underwear. On the way to Beslan, on a country road near the North Ossetian village of Khurikau, they captured an Ingush police officer, Major Sultan Gurazhev. Gurazhev escaped after reaching the town clarification and went to the district police department to inform them that his duty handgun and badge had been stolen from him.

At 0911 hours the hostage takers arrived at Beslan in a GAZelle police van GAZ-66 military truck, manufactured by GAZ a Russian automotive manufacture, which acquired LDV the Birmingham, England based van manufacturer in 2006. They now also produce the Skoda Yeti, Octavia and VW Jetta under licence for VAG in Russia.

Many witnesses and independent experts claim that there were, in fact, two groups of attackers, and that the first group was already at the school when the second group arrived by truck. The first group of hostage takers at the school had supposedly pretended to be repairmen working the school. At first, some staff and students at the school mistook the hostage takers for Russian Special Forces practicing a security drill. However, the hostage takers soon began shooting in the air and forcing everybody within the school grounds, into the main building. During the initial chaos, up to 50 people managed to get out of the school and flee before alerting the authorities. A number of people also managed to hide in the boiler room. After an exchange of gunfire against the police and an armed local civilian, in which reportedly one attacker was killed and two were wounded, the hostage takers seized the school building. The exact number killed in this short but fierce firefight, range from two to eight, and while more than a dozen people were injured.

During the initial siege, the hostage takers took approximately 1,100 hostages, the exact number is hard to calculate due to the number of visitors in the school. The number of hostages was initially downplayed by the government to between 200 and 400, and for an unknown reason announced to be exactly 354. In 2005, their number was put at 1,128. The hostage takers herded their captives into the school's gym and confiscated all their mobile phones under threat of death. They ordered everyone to speak in Russian and only when spoken to. When a father named Ruslan Betrozov stood to calm people and repeat the rules in the local language, Ossetic, a gunman approached him, asked Betrozov if he was done, and shot him in the head. Another father named Vadim Bolloyev, who refused to kneel, was also shot by a captor and bled to death. Their bodies were dragged from the sports hall, leaving a trail of blood later visible in the video made by the hostage-takers.

After gathering the hostages in the gym, the attackers singled out 15–20 of whom they thought were the strongest adults among the male teachers, school employees, and fathers, and took them into a corridor next to the cafeteria on the second floor, where a deadly blast soon took place. An explosive belt on one of the female bombers detonated, killing another female bomber along with several of the selected hostages, as well injuring one male hostage-taker who later died. According to the version presented by the surviving hostage-taker, the blast was actually triggered by the group leader - he set off the bomb by remote control to kill those who openly disagreed about the child hostages and intimidate everyone else. The hostages from this group who were still alive were ordered to lie down and shot with an automatic rifle by another gunman; all but one of them were killed. Karen Mdinaradze, the Alania football team's cameraman, survived the explosion as well as the shooting; when discovered to be still alive, he was allowed to return to the sports hall, where he lost consciousness. The hostage takers, forced other hostages to throw the bodies out of the building and to wash the blood off the floor. One of these hostages, Aslan Kudzayev, escaped by jumping out the window; the authorities briefly detained him as a suspected hostage-taker.

Very quickly a security cordon was soon established around the school, consisting of the Russian police, Internal Troops, Russian Army forces, Spetsnaz, including the elite Alfa and Vympel units of the Russian Federal Security Service (FSB), and the OMON special units of the Russian Ministry of Internal Affairs (MVD). A line of three apartment buildings facing the school gym was evacuated and taken over by the Special Forces. The perimeter they made was within 738ft of the school, inside the range of the militants' grenade launchers. No fire-fighting equipment was in position and, despite the previous experiences of the 2002 Moscow theatre hostage crisis, there were few on ambulances on standby. The chaos outside was worsened by the presence of Ossetian volunteer militiamen (opolchentsy) and armed civilians among the crowds of relatives who had gathered at the scene. Estimates put it at around 5,000.

The hostage takers, placed IEDs in the gym and the rest of the building, and surrounded it with trip wires. In a further bid to deter rescue attempts, they threatened to kill 50 hostages for every one of their own members killed by the police, and to kill 20 hostages for every gunman injured. The hostage takers also threatened to blow up the school if government forces attacked. To avoid being overwhelmed by gas attack like their comrades in the 2002 Moscow hostage crisis, the hostage takers quickly smashed the school's windows. The hostage takers prevented hostages from eating and drinking, until North Ossetia's President Alexander Dzasokhov would arrive to negotiate with them. However, the FSB had set up their own crisis headquarters from which

Dzasokhov was excluded, and threatened to arrest him if he tried to go to the school.

The Russian government announced that it would not use force to rescue the hostages, and negotiations towards a peaceful resolution took place on the first and second days, at first led by Leonid Roshal, a paediatrician whom the hostage-takers had reportedly asked for by name. Roshal had previously helped negotiate the release of children in the 2002 Moscow siege, but also had given advice to the Russian security services as they prepared to storm the theatre, for which he received the Hero of Russia award. The official civilian headquarters was looking for a peaceful resolution of the situation at the same time when the secret "heavy" headquarters set up by the FSB was preparing the assault. Although the FSB restricted what the civilians could do.

At Russia's request, a special meeting of the UN Security Council was convened on the evening of 1 September 2004, at which the council members demanded "the immediate and unconditional release of all hostages of the terrorist attack". President George W. Bush made a statement offering American support to Russia.

On 2 September 2004, day 2 of the siege, negotiations between Roshal and the hostage-takers proved unsuccessful. The hostage takers refused to allow food, water, or medicine to be taken in for the hostages, or for the dead bodies to be removed from the front of the school. At noon, FSB First Deputy Director, Colonel General Vladimir Pronichev showed Dzasokhov a decree signed by Prime Minister Mikhail Fradkov appointing North Ossetian FSB chief Major General Valery Andreyev as head of the operational headquarters.

The Russian government continued to downplay the hostage numbers, repeatedly stating there were only 354 hostages; this reportedly angered the hostage-takers who further mistreated their captives. Several officials also said there appeared to be only 15 to 20 militants in the school. The crisis was met with a near-total silence from the President of Russia, Vladimir Putin and the rest of Russia's political leaders. Only on the second day did Putin make his first public comment on the siege during a meeting in Moscow with King Abdullah II of Jordan in which he said, "Our main task, of course, is to save the lives and health of those who became hostages. All actions by our forces involved in rescuing the hostages will be dedicated exclusively to this task."It was the only public statement by Putin about the crisis until one day after the end of the siege. In protest, to the lack of apparent support from Putin, several people standing outside the school raised signs reading: "Putin! Release our children! Meet their demands!" and "Putin! There are at least 800 hostages!" The locals also said they would not allow any storming or "poisoning of their children" after the poison gas that was used in the 2002 theatre rescue.

Hundreds of hostages were packed into the school gym with wired explosives attached to the basketball hoop. In the afternoon, the gunmen allowed Ruslan Aushev, respected ex-President of Ingushetia and retired Soviet Army general, to enter the school building and agreed to release 11 nursing women and all 15 babies personally to him. The women's older children were left behind and one mother refused to leave, so Aushev carried out her child instead. The rebels gave Aushev a video tape made in the school and a note with demands from their leader, Shamil Basayev, who was not himself present in Beslan. The existence of the note was kept secret by the Russian authorities, while the tape was declared as being empty, even though it was not. It was falsely announced that the hostage takers had made no demands. In the note, Basayev demanded recognition of a "formal independence for Chechnya" in the frame of the Commonwealth of Independent States. He also said that although the Chechen separatists "had played no part" in the Russian apartment bombings of 1999, they would now publicly take responsibility for them if needed. Some Russian officials and state-controlled media later attacked Aushev for entering the school, accusing him of siding with the hostage takers.

The lack of food and water took its toll on the young children, many of whom were forced to stand for long periods in the hot, tightly packed gym. Many children took off their clothing because of the sweltering heat within the gymnasium, which led to rumours of sexual impropriety, though the hostages later explained it was merely due to the stifling heat and being denied any water. Many children fainted, and parents feared they would die. Some hostages even drank their own urine. Occasionally, the hostage takers took out some of the unconscious children and poured water on their heads before returning them to the sports hall. Later in the day, some adults also started to faint from fatigue and thirst. Because of the conditions in the gym, when the explosion and gun battle began on the third day, many of the surviving children were so fatigued that they were barely able to flee from the carnage in their weakened state.

At around 1530 hours, two grenades were detonated approximately ten minutes apart by the hostage takers at security forces outside the school, setting a police car on fire and injuring one officer. The Russian forces did not return fire in case it inflamed the situation. As the day and night wore on, the combination of stress and sleep deprivation along with possibly drug withdrawal made the hostage takers more and more unpredictable, with vast mood violent mood swings. Made the hostage-takers increasingly hysterical and unpredictable. The crying of the children irritated them, and on several occasions crying children and their mothers were threatened with being shot if they would not stop crying. Russian authorities claimed that the hostage-takers had "listened to German heavy metal group Rammstein on personal stereos during the siege to keep themselves edgy and fired up." Overnight, a police officer was injured by shots fired from the school. Talks were broken off, resuming the next day.

Early on the third day, Ruslan Aushev, Alexander Dzasokhov, Taymuraz Mansurov (North Ossetia's Parliament Chairman), and First Deputy Chairman Izrail Totoonti together made contact with Aslan Maskhadov. Totoonti said that both Maskhadov and his Western-based emissary Akhmed Zakayev declared they were ready to fly to Beslan to negotiate with the hostage takers, which was later confirmed by Zakayev. Totoonti said that Maskhadov's sole demand was his safe and easy passage to the school. However, the assault began one hour after the agreement on his arrival was made. He also mentioned that journalists from Al Jazeera television offered for three days to participate in the negotiations and enter the school even as hostages.

Russian presidential advisor and former police general, an ethnic Chechen Aslambek Aslakhanov, was also said, to be close to a breakthrough in the secret negotiations with the hostage takers. By the time he left Moscow on the second day, Aslakhanov had accumulated the names of more than 700 well-known Russian figures who were volunteering to enter the school as hostages in exchange for the release of children. Aslakhanov said the hostage takers agreed to allow him to enter the school the next day at 1500 hours, however this would not happen,due to other events overtaking the meeting.

At around 1300 hours on 3 September 2004, it was agreed to allow four, Ministry of Emergency Situations, medical workers in two ambulances to remove 20 bodies from the school grounds, as well as to bring the corpse of the killed rebel to the school. However, at 1303 hours, when the paramedics approached the school, an explosion was heard from the gymnasium. The hostage-takers opened fire on them, killing two, whilst all the rest of the medical workers sought refuge behind their vehicles.

The second explosion, which sounded quite strange was heard some 22 seconds later. At 1305 hours the fire on the roof of the sports hall started and soon the burning rafters and roofing fell onto the hostages below, many of them injured but still living. Eventually, the entire roof collapsed, turning the room into an inferno. The flames reportedly killed some 160 people, more than half of all hostage fatalities by the end of the operation.

There are only theories as to what caused the explosions. One theory being that an accidental explosion caused by the firing of weapons and storming of the school. One of the bombs hostage takers bombs may have been insecurely attached with adhesive tape and fallen own, causing it to detonate. Another said that a hostage taker had tripped a trip ire and set off a bomb. As soon as the explosion had occurred the armed civilians started shooting even though none of the hostage takers were firing. This led the hostage takers to believe the building was being stormed by security forces. Another version is that a grenade went off, again making the hostage takers believe that the school was being stormed. The final theory came out in 2005, when a federal forces sniper shot a hostage taker, who had their foot on a dead man's switch. When they fell back, their foot moved off the switch, detonating a bomb. Another hostage taker corroborated this theory.

In the current officially approved version, Alexander Torshin, head of the Russian parliamentary commission which concluded its work in December 2006, said the hostage takers had started the firefight by intentionally detonating bombs among the hostages, to the surprise of Russian negotiators and commanders. That statement went beyond previous government accounts, which have typically said the bombs exploded in an unexplained accident. Torshin's 2006 report says the hostage taking was planned as a suicide attack from the beginning and that no storming of the building was prepared in advance.

Part of the sports hall wall was demolished by the explosions, allowing some hostages to escape. Local militia opened fire, and the hostage takers returned fire. A number of hostages were killed in the crossfire. Russian officials say the hostage takers shot, hostages as they ran, and the military fired back. The government stated that once the shooting started, troops had no choice but to storm the building.

Police Lieutenant Colonel Elbrus Nogayev, whose wife and daughter died in the school, said, "I heard a command saying, 'Stop shooting! Stop shooting!'" while other troops' radios said, "Attack!'" As the fighting began, an oil company president and negotiator Mikhail Gutseriyev phoned the hostage-takers; he heard "You tricked us!"

The actual order to start the operation, again has conflicting versions of events with some saying FSB Valery Andreyev and others saying FSB deputy directors Vladimir Pronichev and Vladimir Anisimov - who were actually in charge of the Beslan operation. FSB's Special Operations Center, Colonel General Aleksandr Tikhonov was the one who apparently gave the order to use heavy weapons.

Due to the unprecedented start to the operation, meant the Special Forces had to fight their way into the school in a chaotic firefight. The Special Forces were supported by assault groups of the FSB, T-72 tanks, BTR-80 and a MI-4 attack helicopter. Many local civilians also joined in the firefight, having brought along their own weapons – at least one of the armed volunteers is known to have been killed. At the same time, regular conscripted soldiers reportedly fled the scene as the fighting began. Civilian witnesses claimed that the local police also had panicked, even firing in the wrong direction.

Between three and nine RPO-A Shmel rockets, which is a single-shot, self-contained tube shaped launcher which operates much like an RPG or LAW rocket launchers. It has a maximum range of 600 feet and can have three different warheads, one of which just produces smoke. They were fired from nearby apartments had thermobaric warheads, which generate an intense, high-temperature explosion. The hostage takers fired back at Russian positions with RPGs. A BTR armoured vehicle opened fire with its 14.5x114mm KPV heavy machine gun at windows on the second floor as it drove by, close to the school. T-72s also advanced on the school and were seen firing 125mm shells from its main gun.

Many of the hostages were moved by the hostage takers from the burning sports hall into the other parts of the school, in particular the cafeteria, where they were forced to stand at windows to be used as human shields. Many of these hostages were killed during the exchange of fire, it is estimated that 106 to 110 hostages died after being moved to the cafeteria.

By 1500 hours, two hours after the assault began, Russian troops claimed control of most of the school. However, fighting was still continuing on the grounds as evening fell, including resistance from a group of hostage takers holding out in the school's basement. During the firefight, a group of some 13 hostage takers broke through the military cordon and took refuge nearby. Several of them were believed to have entered a nearby two-story building, which was destroyed by tanks and flamethrowers at around 2100 hours. Another group of hostage takers appeared to head back over the railway, chased by helicopters into the town.

Firefighters, who were called by Andreyev two hours after the fire started, we're not prepared to battle the blaze that raged in the gymnasium. One fire truck crew arrived after two hours at their own initiative, but with only 200 litres of water - being unable to connect to the nearby hydrants any attempt to quell the fire would have been futile. The first attempt to tackle the blaze was at 1528 hours, nearly two and a half hours after the start of the fire. A second fire engine arrived at 1543 hours to help tackle the blaze. Ambulances were also thin on the ground, with many more needed to convey the hundreds of casualties to hospital. Many casualties had to be transported to hospital in private cars. Sporadic explosions and gunfire continued into the night despite reports that all resistance by the hostage takers had been suppressed. It took some 12 hours after the first explosions to quell all the hostage takers. Early the next day Putin ordered the borders of North Ossetia closed while some hostage-takers were apparently still pursued. According to the official version of events, 32 militants participated directly in the seizure, one of whom was taken alive while the rest were killed on spot. The number and identity of hostage takers remains a controversial topic, fuelled by the all too often, contradictory government statements and official documents. The September 2004 government statements said a total of 26–27 militants were killed during the siege. At least four militants, including two women, died prior to the Russian storming of the school.

After the siege had ended many of the injured died in the only hospital in Beslan, which was highly unprepared to cope with the number and severity of casualties. Those that survived with serious injuries were later sent to better equipped facilities in Vladikavkaz. Relatives were not allowed to visit hospitals where the wounded were treated, and doctors were not allowed to use their mobile phones. Bulldozers moved into the school the day after to remove debris and body parts, which were taken to the local garbage dump. Three days after the siege, 180 people were still missing. Many of those that survived suffered varying degrees of PTSD (Post Traumatic Stress Disorder). At least one of the survivors later went on to commit suicide as they were unable to live with the horror of what they had been through.

Russian President Vladimir Putin reappeared publicly during a hurried trip to the Beslan hospital in the early hours of 4 September 2004, to see several of the wounded victims in his only visit to Beslan. After returning to Moscow, he ordered a two-day period of national mourning on 6 to 7 September 2004. In his televised speech, Putin paraphrased Joseph Stalin saying: "We showed ourselves to be weak. And the weak get beaten."

Increased security measures were introduced to Russian cities. More than 10,000 people without proper documents were detained by Moscow police in a "terrorist hunt". The Russian public appeared to be generally supportive of increased security measures. In the wake of Beslan, the government proceeded to toughen laws on terrorism and expand the powers of law enforcement agencies.

In addition, Putin signed a law which replaced the direct election of the heads of the federal subjects of Russia with a system whereby they are proposed by the President of Russia and approved or disapproved by the elected legislative bodies of the federal subjects. In the end 334 hostages were killed, including 154 children, 10 others, 10 Special Forces and 31 hostage takers. It was claimed by locals that over 200 of those killed were found with burns, and 100 or more of them were burned alive. The last reported fatality was Yelena Avdonina a 33 year old librarian, who succumbed to her wounds on 8 December 2006. Over 700 people were thought to have been injured and required treatment. The precise fatalities among the Special Forces is unknown, but it included all three commanders of the assault group. Colonel Oleg Ilyin, Lieutenant Colonel Dmitry Razumovsky of Vympel, and Major Alexander Perov of Alfa. At least 30 commandos suffered serious wounds.

On 17 September 2004, radical Chechen guerilla commander Shamil Basayev, at this time operating autonomously from the rest of the North Caucasian rebel movement, issued a statement claiming responsibility for the Beslan school siege, which was strikingly similar to the Chechen raid on Budyonnovsk in 1995 and the Moscow theatre crisis in 2002, incidents in which hundreds of Russian civilians were held hostage by the Chechen rebels led by Basayev. Basayev said his Riyadus-Salikhin had carried out the attack and also claimed responsibility for a series of terrorist bombings in Russia in the weeks before the Beslan crisis. He said that he originally planned to seize at least one school in either Moscow or Saint Petersburg, but lack of funds forced him to pick North Ossetia. Basayev blamed the Russian authorities for "a terrible tragedy" in Beslan. Basayev claimed that he had miscalculated the Kremlin's determination to end the crisis by all means possible. He said he was "cruelly mistaken" and that he was "not delighted by what happened there", but also added to be "planning more Beslan-type operations in the future because we are forced to do so." However, it was the last major act of terrorism in Russia until 2009, as Basayev was soon persuaded to give up indiscriminate attacks by the new rebel leader Abdul-Halim Sadulayev, who made Basayev his second-in-command, but banned hostage taking, kidnapping for ransom, and operations specifically targeting civilians.

The Chechen separatist leader Aslan Maskhadov immediately denied that his forces were involved in the siege, calling it "a blasphemy" for which "there is no justification". Maskhadov described the perpetrators of Beslan as "madmen" driven out of their senses by Russian acts of brutality. He condemned the action and all attacks against civilians via a statement issued by his envoy Akhmed Zakayev in London, blamed it on what he called a radical local group, and agreed to the North Ossetian proposition to act as a negotiator. Later, he also called on western governments to initiate peace talks between Russia and Chechnya and added to "categorically refute all accusations by the Russian government

that President Maskhadov had any involvement in the Beslan event."
Putin responded that he would not negotiate with "child-killers
Maskhadov was killed by Russian commandos in Chechnya on 8 March
2005. Shamil Basayev, the Chechen rebel leader who took ultimate
responsibility for the attack died in Ingushetia in July 2006. It was
reported that men in black uniforms came in and out from the wooded
area adjacent to the estate that runs to the border of North Ossetia; the
men were carrying boxes, shifting them from one vehicle to another,
when a massive explosion resulted. The explosion is believed to have
killed Basayev. His remains were identified forensically 29 December
2006. In the explosion his body had been scattered over a mile with only
his torso remaining at the centre of the explosion and parts of his false
leg.

Basra Rescue

The 2003 invasion of Iraq, lasted from March 19, 2003 to May 1, 2003, and marked the start of the conflict that later came to be known as the Iraq War, incited under WMD pretext and dubbed Operation Iraqi Freedom by the United States. The invasion saw 21 days of major combat operations, during which a combined force of troops from the United States, the United Kingdom, Australia and Poland, invaded Iraq and deposed the Ba'athist government of Saddam Hussein. The invasion phase consisted primarily of a conventionally-fought war, which ended with the capture of the Iraqi capital of Baghdad. Four countries participated with troops during the initial invasion phase, which lasted from 19 March to 9 April 2003. These were the United States (148,000), United Kingdom (45,000), Australia (2,000) and Poland (194). In preparation for the invasion, 100,000 U.S. troops were assembled in Kuwait by 18 February. The United States supplied the majority of the invading forces, but also received support from Kurdish irregulars in Iraqi Kurdistan. Once the initial invasion was over and Saddam Hussain had been removed, it was time to rebuild Iraq. Coalition forces were still required to help stabilise the country. Special Forces were used to capture key targets in the form of members of the previous Iraqi regime to stand trial.

On 30 January 2005, an election for a government to draft a permanent constitution took place. The lack of widespread Sunni Arab participation and some violence marred the event, in which most of the eligible Kurd and Shia populace participated. After the elections, February, March and April proved to be relatively peaceful months compared with the carnage of November 2004 and January 2005, when insurgent attacks were averaging 30 a day from the average of 70.

However, hopes for a quick end to an insurgency and a withdrawal of U.S. troops were dashed, when May 2005 became Iraq's bloodiest month since the invasion of U.S. forces. Suicide bombers, believed to be mainly disheartened Iraqi Sunni Arabs, Syrians and Saudis, tore through Iraq. Their targets were often Shia gatherings or civilian concentrations mainly of Shias. As a result, over 700 Iraqi civilians died in May, as well as 79 U.S. soldiers; the streets were filled with corpses and the Shias were outraged. It meant Iraq was still very much an unstable country, with the Shia and Sunni groups vying for power and control. All hopes of mass troop withdrawals were dashed and SF operations stepped up to gather intelligence as well as capture key insurgents. There were elements of corruption and infiltration of militants into the security forces.

On 19 September 2005, two SAS soldiers were on a surveillance operation in an unmarked car, close to the Jamiyat police station in Basra, Iraq. The SAS had been tasked with investigating claims that the Iraqi police had been torturing prisoners in the station. One particular senior police officer was suspected, and it was he who the two-man SAS team were watching.

The surveillance team was heading back when their army-supplied car broke down and they had no choice but to get a taxi out of the area. When they reached an army checkpoint, which was believed to be a set-up, they were marched into an outhouse next door, stripped naked, blindfolded and handcuffed before being bundled into a car and taken to a police station. At the station, they were thrown into a cell and tortured with mock executions; a pistol barrel was placed into the backs of their heads and the captors pretended to fire, even though the gun was not loaded. This was one of many mock executions the SAS hostages would endure, carried out by what was thought to be the local militia during the nine hours they were held hostage. One of the prisoners, Colin Maclachlan, had already received a head wound during the arrest. MacLauchlan had been involved in Operation Barras in 2000 and had directly taken part in the rescue of the hostages.

Outside the police station could be heard shouting from rioters, along with gunfire and explosions. A British army, police officer wandered into the station and on hearing his British accent, Maclachlan shouted out that they were SAS soldiers being held hostage. The Iraqi police tried to convince the British officer that they were actually Egyptian terrorists, but the officer was not convinced and went to get help. Troops were sent in, in the form of two warrior tanks. However, the tanks came under attack from petrol bombs, and the crew from one of the tanks, Sgt George Long of the Staffordshire Regiment, had his uniform partially set alight by a petrol bomb. He had no choice but to leap from the tank and roll on the ground to put the flames out. These images were captured by news teams and spread by the media across the world. With the increasingly hostile crowd, the warrior tanks had no choice but to make a tactical withdrawal. The local militia had armed the angry mob with petrol bombs to use against the British forces. The British Embassy had already used its official channels to request the release of the two SAS men. The Iraq interior ministry issued an order for their release but this was duly ignored. A team of SAS were sitting in the back of a C-130 some 130 miles away waiting for the order to go, as the commanders fought to get the green light. The SAS knew the security forces in Jamiat were preparing to withstand an attack. They had men being brought in with rocket-propelled grenades. In the end, the SAS Lieutenant Colonel gave the order to go and was told that he could only mount a rescue mission once it was already in progress. As darkness fell, the SAS went into action in ten armoured vehicles packed with soldiers. On arrival, the tanks bulldozed through the perimeter wall, smashing outbuildings and cars as they did so.

The SAS, having learnt that the captured SAS had been moved from Jamiat to a house round the corner, changed their plans accordingly. They found the house, blew down the door and windows and stormed in, finding no resistance. The two captured SAS soldiers were found in a locked room. The belief was that dickers, the name given for local spies, had probably tipped the kidnappers off to the presence of the SAS. They had fled rather than be killed in a fire fight. The SAS suffered no serious injuries during the raid. However, the Iraqi police demanded compensation, furious that 100 prisoners had escaped and the police station had suffered damage.

Operation Marlborough

Within three weeks during May and June 2005, three Delta Force operators had been killed on operations in Iraq. With Delta Force squadrons fielding only 30 to 40 operators, it was not long before injuries and deaths started to have an impact on their capability. The UK Special Forces were asked to assist, but help was initially refused and another squadron of Delta Force personnel were flown in. However, Delta Force found itself so committed and the intelligence they had needed to be acted upon so urgently that the British Task Force Black in Bagdad was given the job.

Operation Marlborough was hastily put together and was to be undertaken by M Squadron, who were on their second tour of duty in Baghdad. It was the kind of operation that M Squadron had yearned for. There were some members of G Squadron SAS who helped out, but the bulk of the personnel involved were SBS. It was a hot and humid night as the Special Forces assembled for the operation. There was still quite a bit of tension between the SAS and SBS. M Squadron had been mauled in Iraq back in 2003, losing most of its vehicles and equipment. The SAS felt that the SBS were not up to the job and labelled them 'Tier 2 SF'. At the time the SBS was looking to double in size, adding to the tension with the SAS. The SBS undertook the same joint selection process and many recruits had been syphoned off into the growing SBS. The SBS, though, was thought to have less macho swagger and more thoughtfulness than the SAS. Back in 2004, C Squadron had mounted 22 raids compared to the 85 raids A Squadron mounted in their tour in 2003. This made the SBS look laid-back and less able, even though in reality that was not the case. At that point it was down to the UK-US cooperation, where US SF would often get more and bigger operations and British SF would at times be sidelined.

The team for Operation Marlborough consisted of 16 mainly SBS soldiers, including four SBS sniper teams, each armed with .338 Lapua Magnum chambered L115A AWM sniper rifles. Escape routes were watched by the remaining members of the group in case of immediate emergency or escape if and when needed. The sniper team's mission was to kill Al-Qaeda terrorists wearing suicide vests laden with explosives. They later planned to detonate these vests in densely packed cafes and restaurants frequented by members of the Iraqi security forces. This intelligence had been obtained by Iraqi double agents working for both the British and US Secret Intelligence Services.

On 23 July 2005, the SBS arrived close to their target house, labelled Alpha, with a combination of Humvees and Puma helicopters. US personnel were also closely involved, with a detachment of Rangers acting as a backup force. Some M1 tanks had also been brought in as backup as the operation was in a dangerous neighbourhood. Overhead Task Force Black had Puma helicopters circling, carrying snipers in case the occupants of Alpha tried to launch an attack. A United States predator UAV circled above and had the target building under video surveillance, sending its imagery back to the Task Force Black Headquarters. Listening devices had already been laid inside the building and were being monitored by Arabic-speaking translators. Finally, a command and control aircraft also orbited ahead, linking all the various forces together through a single command. As the SBS moved forward towards their target, a man wearing a suicide vest came running out at them. He detonated his bomb, but it was too early to kill any of the SBS who had quickly taken cover and were crouching down when the vest detonated. The blast caused one of the Pumas that was circling about 100 feet above to rise up in the blast wave before dropping like a stone, trying to find some good air. The pilot, even at the low altitude the helicopter was at, managed to recover by winding up the engines to max power, and he started to pull up within feet of a rooftop. There was no time to dwell as the operation was picking up pace. Another of the airborne platforms had picked up via its image-intensifying camera a man leaving the back of a building and making a run for it. The circling Puma swung round to give the SBS sniper a chance to line up a shot. He lined him up in his sights before squeezing off a round that killed the man instantly. He was subsequently found to be another suicide bomber.

Alpha was now ready to be stormed by the SBS, who burst through the front door and conducted room by room clearance. As they went in, another man wearing a suicide vest ran towards them. One of the SBS opened up on him at close range, dropping him. He had been shot down before he had a chance to activate the bomb and lay slumped up against a blood-splattered wall. The SBS slowly made their way with a little trepidation, fearing that another suicide bomber may make another run for them. This time they may not be quite so lucky. Many of the rooms contained bomb parts and explosives, which meant a grenade could not be thrown in for fear of setting all the explosives off. It was a slow process and no further suicide bombers were found. The SBS withdrew and the bomb disposal experts moved in. The SBS was commended for experiencing what Delta Force operatives had been experiencing as they hunted down Al-Qaeda cells.

The Puma helicopter pilot who had shown expert airmanship and rescued his bird was decorated for his airmanship. The SBS had proven that they were just as good as the SAS and Delta Force when taking on Al-Qaeda.

Operation Neptune Spear

Osama bin Laden was the founder and head of the Islamist militant group Al-Qaeda. The Americans had been hunting him down for nearly ten years following the 9/11 attacks. They had got close to him several times, with an SBS team actually being pretty sure they had spotted him being carried towards the border of Pakistan from Afghanistan in 2001. They were within striking distance, but were told to stand down and wait for American Special Forces to arrive. By the time they got there, the opportunity to capture Osama bin Laden had been lost. Only two days after the September 11 attacks, the US President at the time, George W. Bush, said, "The most important thing is for us to find Osama bin Laden." He added, "It is our number one priority and we will not rest until we find him." The search continued and all possible leads were followed but with very little success. Four months after President Obama came to power, he sent a memo to the CIA asking them to provide within 30 days a detailed plan for locating Osama bin Laden and bringing him to justice. The intelligence agencies' effort to locate Bin Laden came from a small piece of information unearthed in 2002, which drove the investigation forward over subsequent years. It was at the start of September 2010 that a lead helped them discover Osama bin Laden at a compound in Abbottabad, Pakistan. A wiretap of another suspect picked up a conversation with Abu Ahmed al-Kuwaiti. CIA paramilitary operatives located al-Kuwaiti in August 2010 and followed him back to the Abbottabad compound, which led to the speculation that Bin Laden was there. This led to an extensive surveillance operation of the compound. The CIA studied hundreds of intelligence photos of the inhabitants, along with intelligence reports to determine the identities of all those present. The conclusion was drawn that Bin Laden was living there with his young wife and family.

The actual compound bin Laden was living in had been built in 2004. It was a three-story building situated at the end of a narrow dirt road, with two security gates and surrounded by high walls topped with barbed wire. The compound's location was only about 100 miles from the Afghan border and under a mile away from the Pakistani military academy. The compound had no telephone or internet links. The occupants would burn all their rubbish rather than put it out for collection like their neighbours. The CIA rented a home in Abbottabad in order to stake out the compound over a period of a few months. All the information collected would be later used to prepare for the Special Forces' raid. The compound, due to its design, made it very easy to observe and was one of the reasons Bin Laden was discovered.

The operation to kill or capture Bin Laden was called Operation Neptune Spear. The feeling was that it would more than likely end in a kill as the occupants, including Bin Laden, were unlikely to simply surrender. Full authority was however given to kill Bin Laden if the need arose, although there have been conflicting reports that the operation was a 'kill' operation. The CIA briefed Vice Admiral William H. McRaven, the commander of the JSOC (Joint Special Operations Command), about the compound in January 2011. McRaven thought a commando raid would be pretty straightforward; the main concern was the Pakistani response to the raid as they would not be consulted for fear of Bin Laden being tipped off. The raid was planned from the CIA's Langley compound by seven JSOC officers. The planners considered various options, including using B2 Stealth bombers to attack the compound. A joint operation with Pakistan forces was also considered, but fears of leaks from the Pakistani military or government put too big a risk on operational security. On 14 March 2011, President Obama met with the NSC (National Security Council) to review all the options. There was still a view that Bin Laden was not at the compound and a commando raid was far too risky. The President was leaning towards a B2 bombing raid. To this end, the US Air Force was tasked with looking into this option further. One of the issues with a bombing raid was that the CIA was unable to rule out the possibility that the compound had an underground bunker. This meant that a 910kg JDAM (Joint Direct Attack Munition) bomb would be required to destroy it and the blast radius would be within range of at least one other house. Estimates put it that as well as the occupants of the compound, up to 12 other civilians could be killed. The next issue was being able to confirm that Bin Laden was indeed dead and had not survived, as the evidence remaining after the bomb had exploded would not likely be enough to confirm or deny that Bin Laden had been killed. On 28th March, at the next Security Council meeting, President Obama put the bombing plan on hold. Instead, he got Admiral McRaven to develop the plan for a helicopter raid. At the same time, the US intelligence community studied the option of taking Bin Laden out with a drone that could fire small tactical munitions as he paced in his compound's vegetable garden.

A team was assembled by McRaven using a team from Red Squadron, who was coming home from Afghanistan and could be re-directed without drawing any attention. The team that was assembled had the experience and language skills needed for cross border operations into Pakistan. The team was not told of their actual objective, even though they carried out rehearsals in a mock-up of the compound at the Harvey Testing Activity facility in North Carolina. The other training location was in Nevada at 4000 feet, reflecting the effects of altitude on the helicopters. However, the mock-up in Nevada used a chain-link fence instead of a wall, so the effects on lift to the helicopters with the high walls around Bin Laden's compound were not realised.

Those planning the mission believed that the SEALs could get in and out of Abbottabad without being challenged. They were to use specially developed UH-60 Black Hawk helicopters which had been designed to be quiet and stealthy by the fitting of various steal technologies, including low radar absorbent paint and a new tail rotor that looked very similar in appearance to the one that was fitted to the cancelled Comanche helicopter. The engine exhaust was muffled and again made stealthy. It helped that the Americans had assisted in training and equipping the Pakistanis, so their defensive capabilities were known. The Americans had also supplied F16 aircraft with the condition that they had 24-hour surveillance by the US. This meant that if they were scrambled to intercept, the US would know about it before the F16s had even taken off. If Bin Laden was captured, he was to be taken and held just outside Bagram airbase in Afghanistan. Contingency plans were also put in place in case the SEAL team was discovered by the Pakistanis during the raid.

At the next NSC meeting on 19 April, President Obama gave provisional approval for the helicopter raid. He was still concerned about the contingency plan if the SEAL team was discovered by the Pakistanis, and wanted the SEAL team equipped to fight its way out if needed. Not long after that meeting, McRaven and his SEAL team left for Afghanistan to do further practice raids in a restricted area of Bagram called Camp Alpha. Again, a full-size mock-up of the compound was constructed to practice on. The final plan was explained to the NSC on

28 April, and to enable the SEAL team to fight their way out, Chinooks helicopters were equipped with M134 Miniguns and extra fuel for the Black Hawks. An additional SEAL team would also be available as a QRF (Quick Reaction Force). All of these extra assets would be stationed just across the border in Afghanistan. Most of the NSC was in support of the raid; only Vice President Biden was opposed and still wanted the use of a drone instead, although he gave his support to the helicopter raid the very next day. President Obama had a chat with McRaven to see if he had any final doubts, to which he replied, "No." The final 'go-ahead' for the raid was given on 29 April for the raid to take place the next day (although it ended up being delayed by a day due to cloudy weather).

On 1 May 2011, McRaven was given the order to move forward with the operation. The President would watch the raid from the Situation Room with other national security officials. All the military personnel involved in the mission were temporarily transferred to the control of the civilian Central Intelligence Agency. This was for legal reasons, as America was not at war with Pakistan.

The SEALs would operate in two teams and were equipped with Heckler & Koch 416 carbine military assault rifles and Heckler & Koch MP7s weapons with suppressors attached. The SEALs also had night-vision goggles, body armour and handguns as backup weapons. As well as the SEALs, a dog was used to enable the tracking of anyone who escaped and to alert the SEALs of any approaching Pakistani forces. The dog could also be used as a deterrent for Pakistani security forces, as well as help look for any hidden rooms or doors within the compound.

The SEALs flew into Pakistan from a staging base in the city of Jalalabad in eastern Afghanistan. The raid had been scheduled when there was the least amount of moonlight to help the Black Hawks enter Pakistan undetected. They would also be supported by other fighter and support aircraft, along with drones. As the helicopters flew into Pakistan, they made use of the hilly terrain to fly nap-of-the-earth to ensure they reached the compound without being spotted on radar. Their flight from Jalalabad to Abbottabad took around 90 minutes. Their Black Hawks had no seats, just the odd collapsible garden chair to reduce weight; the SEAL team was crammed inside with very little space to move. On arrival, some of the local residents heard the helicopters overhead and they were able to see much of the raid. The first helicopter came in to hover, ready for the SEALs to jump off. The pilot had done this kind of manoeuvre many times before, and to him it was almost like parking a car. As the helicopter hovered, it kicked up the dust from the ground below and caused the laundry on the washing lines to flail about. The helicopter started to experience a hazardous airflow condition known as a vortex ring state. This was due to the high temperatures, high altitude and the compound walls, which prevented the rotor downwash from diffusing. As the helicopter became unstable it started to rock, gently at first, but becoming more pronounced as the pilot struggled to keep it stable. The helicopter was veering between the guest house and the compound wall as it struggled to find enough air to remain airborne. The pilot had no choice but to regain height and land outside the compound. As it tried to gain height it turned left, just missing the guesthouse, before swinging round; its tail grazed one of the compound walls, damaging the it and tail rotor. This in turn caused the helicopter to start turning on its side. The pilot countered this by burying the nose of the helicopter into the ground to prevent it from tipping over. As it was a soft crash landing, none of the SEALs or aircrew was injured. The helicopter was pitched at a 45-degree angle next to the compound wall.

The second helicopter decided to land outside the compound, and the SEALs had to scale the high compound walls to get in before advancing into the house. They breached walls and doors with explosives. As the SEALs moved forward, they encountered residents in the guest house. Al-Kuwaiti opened fire on the SEALs with an AK-47 from behind the guesthouse door; a small fire fight ensued in which al-Kuwaiti was killed. His wife is also believed to have been injured during the exchange of fire. As the second SEAL team entered the first floor in the main house, they encountered Abrar, who was shot and killed. At the same time, his wife Bushra was killed by the advancing SEAL team. The young son of Bin Laden rushed towards the SEAL team on the staircase in the main house and was promptly shot and killed. SEALs had to make split second decisions about whether or not these individuals presented an immediate risk. Unsure of hidden weapons or even the use of suicide vests, the safest option was to kill rather than be killed. It may have been that in the pitch dark after CIA operatives had cut power, Bin Laden's son was simply fleeing in terror. The SEAL team located Bin Laden on the third floor; he was wearing loose-fitting tunic and trousers. These trousers, when studied later, were found to have $500 and two phone numbers sewn into the fabric. Bin Laden peered over the third floor ledge at the advancing SEALs; as soon as he was spotted, he fled back into his room as the SEALs fired a volley of shots. The SEALs, hot on Bin Laden's heels, burst into his room. Bin Laden was on the floor with a head wound and one of his wives stood shielding him. One of the wives, Amal Ahmed, screamed at the SEALs in Arabic and looked as if she was about to charge at them. The first SEAL through the door shot her in the leg, before grabbing both women and pushing them aside. A second SEAL entered the room before two more shot Bin Laden in the chest with an H&K 416 assault rifle. It was thought that he was about to get up and grab the AKSU-74, a shortened version of the AKS-74 assault rifle, which was situated above the headboard on his bed. Bin Laden lay dead and the SEAL team leader radioed through, "For God and country—Geronimo, Geronimo, Geronimo." McRaven prompted the SEAL team leader for confirmation that Bin Laden was dead and this was followed by "Geronimo E.K.I.A." E.K.I.A means 'Enemy Killed in Action.' Weapons were found in Bin Laden's room, although there were conflicting reports that he was shot before he had a chance to reach his AKSU or even the pistol that was later found in his room.

As the SEALs swept the house, many women and children were found with their wrists bound with plastic handcuffs or zip ties. Once the raid was complete, the SEALs moved all the residents outside for the Pakistani forces to discover along with the rest of the residents of the compound - one woman and three men killed in the raid. Their bodies were also left for the Pakistanis to deal with. Only Bin Laden's body was taken away. Those killed by the SEALs were Bin Laden's courier, Abu Ahmed al-Kuwaiti, al-Kuwaiti's brother Abrar, Abrar's wife Bushra, and Bin Laden's adult son Khalid. The raid had taken 38 minutes from start to finish, with the first 15 minutes completing the military aspect. The rest of the time was spent room-to-room clearing, securing women and children, searching the compound for information, and clearing weapon stashes and barricades. Along with intelligence and weapons, a large stash of opium was also found.

The helicopter that had crashed and was no longer flyable needed to be destroyed to keep it classified. The pilot smashed important instruments in the cockpit before the SEALs planted explosives and blew it up. Now with only one helicopter, the two Chinooks held in reserve were called forward to transport the SEALs and Bin Laden's body back to Afghanistan and Bagram airfield. Once at Bagram, Bin Laden's body was flown on a V-22 Osprey escorted by two F/A 18 hornets back to the aircraft carrier, Carl Vinson. The reason for the burial of bin Laden being undertaken at sea was that no country would accept his body. It was the Saudi government that approved his sea burial following full Muslim rites. Before his burial, several DNA samples and photos were taken to ensure they had indeed got Bin Laden. They also measured the corpse's length to see if it matched Bin Laden's tall stature (6ft 4in). Facial recognition software was used and came back with a 90 to 95% likely match. One of his wives also identified the body, although she was still reeling from the way the SEALs had executed her husband.

News of the raid was not shared with the Pakistani government until after it was over. It was confirmed that the F16s were scrambled after they became aware of the raid, but by the time they got to the compound, the helicopters had left.

The reports of Bin Laden's death on 1 May were not universally accepted and many conspiracy theories began to pop up, despite the death having been witnessed by bin Laden's 12-year-old daughter. Then, on 6 May, al-Qaeda issued a statement confirming his death. The swift burial of Bin Laden's body at sea, the speed of the DNA results, and the decision not to release pictures of the body led to the rise of conspiracy theories that Bin Laden had not died in the raid after all. But nothing can be taken away from the Navy SEALs' part in a daring and tenacious raid that will go down in history. Pakistan was accused of harbouring Bin Laden, although there is no real proof that they had any idea he was hiding there. A major terrorist player had been removed and the hope was that this would help reduce Al-Qaeda's influence around the world.

Operation Thalathine

Piracy off the coast of Somalia has been a threat to international shipping since the second phase of the Somali Civil War. Since 2005, a number of international organizations, including the International Maritime Organization and the World Food Programme, have expressed concern over the rise in acts of piracy. Piracy has impeded the delivery of shipments and increased shipping expenses, costing an estimated $6.6 to $6.9 billion a year in global trade. After the collapse of the central government in the ensuing civil war, the Somali Navy disbanded. With Somali territorial waters undefended, foreign fishing trawlers began illegally fishing on the Somali seaboard and ships from big companies started dumping waste off the coast of Somalia. This led to the erosion of the fish stock. Local fishermen subsequently started to band together to protect their resources. After seeing the potential of making money out of ransom payments, some financiers and former militiamen later began to fund pirate activities, splitting the profits evenly with the pirates.

Operation Ocean Shield was NATO's contribution to Operation Enduring Freedom - Horn of Africa (OEF-HOA), an anti-piracy initiative in the Indian Ocean, following the earlier Operation Allied Protector. Naval operations began on 17 August 2009 after being approved by the North Atlantic Council.

In April 20008, a French three mastered luxury yacht called Le Ponant, operating as a cruise ship for up to 67 passengers in 32 cabins was on the high seas. While the ship was sailing through the Gulf of Aden on 4 April 2008 with a crew of 30. It was travelling from the Seychelles islands to the Mediterranean, when it was seized by six Somali pirates armed with AK-47s. The pirates from the village of Garaad-Ade, had earlier seized a Yemeni trawler, which had a crew of 27 and used this trawler as the mother ship to mount further attacks from. The crew of the yacht was not alarmed as the trawler closed in on them, and were alerted, only when three armed men mounted a speed boat from the trawler. The crew of the yacht had planned to fight them off, until the pirates opened fire with AK-47s. The crew of the yacht decided to surrender and the three pirates boarded the yacht, shortly followed by a further six pirates. The yacht, headed for Garaad-Ade with both of the pirate boats in tow. Once at Garaad-Ade, 30 of the 90 villagers took it in turns to guard the yacht. The pirates demanded a ransom thought to be around 2 million US dollars from the yacht owners for the release of the yacht and crew.

Anti-piracy forces, including the French naval sloop Commandant Bouan and a Sikorsky CH-124 Sea King helicopter from the Canadian destroyer Charlottetown, had kept watch on the yacht after it had been seized. They had been alerted by the yacht captain. After the ransom had been paid, the yacht was released along with most of her crew members taken on board the Commandant Boua.

After the hostage release, French naval helicopters, tracked the pirates as they moved to the village of Jariban. During this period the French had alerted the Groupe'd' Intervention de la Gendarmerie Nationale born out of the Munic Olympic games massacre and a prison mutiny Clairvaux prison the year before. Commonly abbreviated GIGN is a special operations unit of the French Armed Forces. It is part of the National Gendarmerie and is trained to perform counter-terrorist and hostage rescue missions in France or anywhere else in the world. The GIGN was formed in 1973. On 1 September 2007, a major reorganization took place. The original GIGN absorbed the Gendarmerie Parachute Squadron (EPIGN) and the thirty gendarmes of the GSPR to form a "new" expanded GIGN. There are now three distinct parts to the unit, Intervention force (the original GIGN), Observation & search force (from the former EPIGN), Security & protection force (from the former EPIGN and gendarmes from the GSPR). The capture of the pirates was called operation Thalathine.

Operating from the frigate Jean Bart and helicopter cruiser Jeanne d'Arc elements of the GIGN supported by French Naval commandos moved in when pirates attempted to flee into the desert. A Marine Commando sniper fired a shot into the engine disabling the getaway car. Three commandos from a Gazelle helicopter went in and arrested the six pirates, recovering 200,000 dollars. The rest had most likely gone to various pirate leaders, that pointed to a much or coordinated operation. The pirates initially did not want to come quietly and a couple of bursts of fire over their heads got them lying face down on the desert. The six pirates were taken back to France to face trial. On 16 September 2009, the Court of Cassation placed charges against six Somalis accused of hostage-taking of the yacht Le Ponant in April 2008, the lawyers pleaded that it was an illegal charge. Lawyers for the six suspected pirates, believed that their clients had been held outside any legal framework between their arrest on 11 April on Somali territory and their placement in custody five days later. The Court of Cassation, stated that French law applied despite their arrest in Somalia but its retention on board a military vessel outside any legal framework for five days was associated with a "circumstance insurmountable," in other words was something that had to be undertaken and could not have been done any other way. The Supreme Court has held that this did not justify the cancellation of the procedure, and that the pirates could be charged.

Libyan Civil War 2011

Libya is in the Maghreb region of North Africa bordered by the Mediterranean Sea to the north, Egypt to the east, Sudan to the southeast, Chad and Niger to the south, and Algeria and Tunisia to the west. The three traditional parts of the country are Tripolitania, Fezzan and Cyrenaica. With an area of almost 1.8 million square kilometres (700,000 sq mi), which makes Libya the 17th largest country in the world. Its capital is which has around 1.7 million of the country's 6.4 million inhabitants. It has large oil reserves that have helped to give Libya high GDP. It is a country that has seen many wars and was a key area during the North Africa Desert campaign in the Second World War. Colonel Muammar Gaddafi ruled Libya for 42 years from 1 September 1969 to 23 August 2011.

The discovery of significant oil reserves in 1959 and the income that came from petroleum sales enabled the Kingdom of Libya to transition from one of the world's poorest nations to a wealthy state. The oil drastically improved the Libyan government's finances, although this was not fully passed onto the Libyan people and resent began to build over the increased concentration of the nation's wealth in the hands of King Idris. The increasing discontent rose with the rise of Nasserism and Arab nationalism/socialism throughout North Africa and the Middle East. Then on the 1 September 1969, a group of that consisted of 70 young army officers known as the Free Officers Movement along with enlisted men, mostly assigned to the Signal Corps, seized control of the government. In a single stroke they abolished the Libyan monarchy. The coup was launched from Benghazi, and within a couple hours they had taken control of government. Army units quickly rallied in support of the coup, so that within a matter of days military control was established in Tripoli and elsewhere throughout the country. The coup was received enthusiastically, especially by the younger generation living in the urban areas of Libya. Any fears of resistance in Cyrenaica and Fezzan quickly proved unfounded.

Credit for carrying out the coup was claimed by the Free Officers Movement. The Free Officers Movement was headed by a twelve-member directorate that designated itself the Revolutionary Command Council (RCC). The RCC constituted the Libyan government after the coup.

In its initial proclamation on 1 September, the RCC declared the country to be a free and sovereign state called the Libyan Arab Republic. Which would proceed, "in the path of freedom, unity, and social justice, guaranteeing the right of equality to its citizens, and opening before them the doors of honourable work". The rule of the Turks and Italians and the "reactionary" government just overthrown were characterised as belonging to "dark ages", from which the Libyan people were called to move forward as "free brothers" to a new age of prosperity, equality, and honour. The RCC advised that the coup had not been directed from outside and would ensure that existing treaties and agreements would remain in effect, and that foreign lives and property would be protected. Diplomatic recognition of the new government came quickly from countries throughout the world. The United States recognition of the new government was officially extended on 6 September 1969. With such little internal resistance, the fear was that a possible reaction by the absent King Idris or his designated heir, Hasan ar Rida. They had been taken into custody at the time of the coup along with other senior civil and military officials of the royal government may follow. However, within days of the coup, Hasan publicly renounced all rights to the throne and stated his support for the new government. He called on the people to accept it without violence. Idris, in an exchange of messages with the RCC through Egypt's President Nasser, dissociated himself from reported attempts to secure British intervention and disclaimed any intention of coming back to Libya. In return, he was assured by the RCC of the safety of his family still in the country. At his own request and with Nasser's approval, Idris took up residence once again in Egypt, where he remained until his death in 1983.

On 7 September 1969, the RCC made an announcement that it had appointed a cabinet to conduct the government of the new republic. An American-educated technician, Mahmud Sulayman al-Maghribi, who had been imprisoned since 1967 for his political activities, was designated prime minister. He presided over the eight-member Council of Ministers, of whom six, like Maghrabi, were civilians and two – Adam Said Hawwaz and Musa Ahmad – were military officers. Neither of the officers was a member of the RCC. The Council of Ministers was instructed to "implement the state's general policy as drawn up by the RCC", making sure there was no doubt where the ultimate authority lay.

The next day the RCC decided to promote Captain Muammar Gaddafi to colonel and also appoint him commander in chief of the Libyan Armed Forces. Although RCC spokesmen declined until January 1970 to reveal any other names of RCC members, it was apparent from that date onward that the head of the RCC and the new head of state was Colonel Muammar Gaddafi.

It was quickly pointed out by analysts of the striking similarities between the Egypt coup under Nasser in 1952 and the Libyan military coup of 1969. It soon became clear that the Egyptian experience and Nasser had formed the model for the Free Officers Movement. As the RCC in the last months of 1969 moved quickly to apply domestic reforms, it proclaimed neutrality in the confrontation between the superpowers and opposition to all forms of colonialism and "imperialism". It also made clear of Libya's dedication to Arab unity and to the support of the Palestinian cause against Israel. The RCC reaffirmed the country's identity as part of the "Arab nation" and its state religion as Islam. It abolished parliamentary institutions, all legislative functions being assumed by the RCC, and continued the prohibition against political parties that had been in effect since 1952. The new government categorically rejected communism – in a large part because it was atheist – and officially espoused an Arab interpretation of socialism that integrated Islamic principles with social, economic, and political reform. Libya had shifted, virtually overnight, from the camp of conservative Arab traditional. From 1969 to 1977 there were further attempts of coups. Following the formation of the Libyan Arab Republic, Gaddafi and his associates insisted that their government would not rest on individual leadership, but rather on collegial decision making. The first major cabinet change occurred soon after the first challenge to the government. On December 1969, Adam Said Hawwaz, the minister of defence, and Musa Ahmad, the minister of interior, were arrested and accused of planning a coup. In the new cabinet formed after the crisis, Gaddafi, retaining his post as chairman of the RCC, also became prime minister and defence minister. Major Abdel Salam Jallud, generally regarded as second only to Gaddafi in the RCC, became deputy prime minister and minister of interior. This cabinet totalled thirteen members, of whom five were RCC officers. The government was challenged a second time in July 1970 when Abdullah Abid Sanusi and

Ahmed al-Senussi, distant cousins of former King Idris, and members of the Sayf an Nasr clan of Fezzan were accused of plotting to seize power for themselves. After the plot was foiled, a substantial cabinet change occurred, RCC officers for the first time forming a majority among new ministers. From the start, RCC spokesmen had indicated a serious intent to bring the "defunct regime" to account. In 1971 and 1972 more than 200 former government officials—including seven prime ministers and numerous cabinet ministers—as well as the former King Idris and members of the royal family, were brought to trial on charges of treason and corruption in the Libyan People's Court. Many, who like Idris lived in exile, were tried in absentia. Although a large percentage of those charged were acquitted, sentences of up to fifteen years in prison and heavy fines were imposed on others. Five death sentences, all but one of them in absentia, were pronounced, among them, one against Idris. Fatima, the former queen, and Hasan ar Rida were sentenced to five and three years in prison, respectively.

Meanwhile, Gaddafi and the RCC had disbanded the Sanusi order and officially downgraded its historical role in achieving Libya's independence. He also attacked regional and tribal differences as obstructions in the path of social advancement and Arab unity, dismissing traditional leaders and drawing administrative boundaries across tribal groupings.

The Free Officers Movement was renamed "Arab Socialist Union" (ASU) in 1971, modelled after Egypt's Arab Socialist Union, and made the sole legal party in Gaddafi's Libya. It acted as a "vehicle of national expression", purporting to "raise the political consciousness of Libyans as well as aiding the RCC in formulating public policy through debate in open forums. Trade unions were incorporated into the ASU and strikes outlawed. The press, already subject to censorship, was officially conscripted in 1972 as an agent of the revolution. Italians and what remained of the Jewish community were expelled from the country and their property confiscated in October 1970.

In 1972, Libya joined the Federation of Arab Republics with Egypt and Syria, but the intended union of pan-Arab states ended up not being the success that was hoped for, and was effectively dormant after 1973.

As months passed, Colonel Gaddafi, caught up in his apocalyptic visions of revolutionary pan-Arabism and Islam locked in mortal struggle with what he termed the encircling, the demonic forces of reaction, imperialism, and Zionism, increasingly spent his time dealing with international rather than internal affairs. As a result, routine administrative tasks fell to Major Jallud, who in 1972 became prime minister in place of Gaddafi. Two years later Jallud assumed Gaddafi's remaining administrative and protocol duties to allow Gaddafi to devote his time to revolutionary theorizing. Gaddafi remained commander in chief of the armed forces and effective head of state. The foreign press speculated about an eclipse of his authority and personality within the RCC, but Gaddafi soon dispelled such theories by his measures to restructure Libyan society.

After the September coup, U.S. forces proceeded deliberately with the planned withdrawal from Wheelus Air Base under the agreement made by the previous government. The last of the American contingent turned the facility over to the Libyans on 11 June 1970, a date thereafter celebrated in Libya as a national holiday. As relations with the U.S. steadily deteriorated, Gaddafi forged close links with the Soviet Union and other Eastern Bloc countries, all the while maintaining Libya's stance as a nonaligned country and opposing the spread of communism in the Arab world. Libya's army—sharply increased from the 6,000-man prerevolutionary force that had been trained and equipped by the British—was armed with Soviet-built armour and missiles. Libya tried to get hold of nuclear missiles from China and Pakistan in the 1970s but to no avail. The relationship with the west, especially America deteriorated further during the 1970s and into the 1980s with various ongoing disputes. On 19 August 1981, a naval dogfight occurred over the Gulf of Sidra in the Mediterranean Sea after Sukhoi Su-22 'Fitter' fired on a pair of U.S. Navy F-14 Tomcat jets. They fired back with AIM-9L Sidewinders; missiles against the formation of Libyan fighter jets in a dogfight and shot down two of the Libyan Su-22 attack aircraft. This naval action was a result of claiming the territory and losses from the previous incident. Again, a second dogfight happened on 4 January 1989; U.S. Navy carrier-based jets also shot down two Libyan MiG-23 Flogger-Es in the same place, adding up to a disastrous loss of the enemy's air force.

A similar action took place on 23 March 1986; while patrolling the Gulf, U.S. naval forces attacked a sizable enemy naval force and various

SAM sites defending Gaddafi's territory. U.S. fighter jets and fighter-bombers destroyed SAM launching facilities and sank various naval vessels, killing 35 seamen. This was a reprisal for the terrorist hijackings between June and December 1985. On 5 April 1986, Libyan agents bombed "La Belle" nightclub in West Berlin, killing three and injuring 229. Gaddafi's plan was intercepted by several national intelligence agencies and more detailed information was retrieved four years later from Stasi archives. The Libyan agents who had carried out the operation, from the Libyan embassy in East Germany, were prosecuted by the reunited Germany in the 1990s. In response to the discotheque bombing, joint United States Air Force, Navy and Marine Corps airstrikes took place against Libya on 15 April 1986 and code-named Operation El Dorado Canyon and known as the 1986 bombing of Libya. The attack began at 0200 hours (Libyan time), and lasted about twelve minutes, with 60 tons of munitions dropped. Eighteen F-111 bombers supported by four EF-111 electronic countermeasures aircraft flying from the United Kingdom bombed Tripoli airfield, a frogman training centre at a naval academy, and the Bab al-Azizia barracks in Tripoli. During the bombing of the Bab al-Azizia barracks, an American F-111 was shot down by a Libyan surface-to-air missile (SAM) over the Gulf of Sidra. Some bombs landed off-target, striking diplomatic and civilian sites in Tripoli, while the French embassy was only narrowly missed. Some Libyan soldiers abandoned their positions in fright and confusion, and officers were slow to give orders. The Libyan anti-aircraft fire did not begin until after the planes had passed over their targets. Twenty-four A-6 Intruders and F/A-18 Hornets launched from aircraft carriers bombed radar and antiaircraft sites in Benghazi before bombing the Benina and Jamahiriya barracks. A number of bombs missed their targets and hit residential areas, along with a number of Western embassies in Benghazi.

Following the 1986 bombing of Libya, Gaddafi intensified his support for anti-American government organisations. He financed Jeff Forts Al-Rukn faction of the Chicago Black P. Stones gang, in their emergence as an indigenous anti-American armed revolutionary movement. Members of Al-Rukn were arrested in 1986 for preparing to conduct strikes on behalf of Libya, including blowing up U.S. government buildings and bringing down an airplane; the Al-Rukn defendants were convicted in

1987 of "offering to commit bombings and assassinations on U.S. soil for Libyan payment." In 1986, Libyan state television announced that Libya was training suicide squads to attack American and European interests. He began financing the IRA again in 1986, to retaliate against the British for harbouring American fighter planes. The downing of Pan Am Flight 103 over Lockerbie in Scotland on the 21 December 1988 would eventually be traced back to Libya and Gadaffi. In 2003, Gaddafi accepted responsibility for the Lockerbie bombing and paid compensation to the families of the victims, although he maintained never having given the order for the attack. During the 2011 civil war, it was mooted that Gaddafi had ordered the bombing of Flight 103.

Gaddafi was removed from power during the civil war and killed by his own people. The civil war in Libya began after the Arab Spring movements overturned the rulers of Tunisia, Libya and Egypt experienced a full-scale revolt beginning on 17 February 2011. The war was preceded by protests in Benghazi, beginning on Tuesday, 15 February 2011, which led to clashes with security forces that fired on the crowd. The protests escalated into a rebellion that spread across the country. By 20 February 2011, the unrest had spread to Tripoli. On 27 February 2011, the National Transitional Council (NTC) was established to administer the areas of Libya under rebel control. The liberation of Libya was celebrated on 23 October 2011, three days after the fall of Sirte. Around 30,000 Libyans died during the civil war.

With the Libyan Civil war in full swing the world initially stood back whilst decisions were about the best way to deal with the civil war. Should the world intervene and support the rebel government. The US was very keen to see Gaddafi be removed from power. With agreements in place, on 19 March 2011, a multi-state coalition began a military intervention in Libya to implement United Nations Security Council Resolution 1973, which was taken in response to events during the Libyan civil war, and military operations began, with US and British naval forces firing over 110 Tomahawk cruise missiles, the French Air Force, British Royal Air Force, and Royal Canadian Air Force undertaking sorties across Libya and a naval blockade by Coalition forces. Airstrikes against Libyan Army tanks and vehicles by French jets. With the air war in full swing British Special Forces in Libya had been in Libya before airstrikes are even begun. Special Forces were used to help train and co-ordinate the rebel forces to become a more effective team to finally topple a Gaddafi's regime. It was not an easy task for the Special Forces as they faced many legal and political constraints imposed from London. Special Forces worked closely with the NTC and contributed to the final collapse of the Gaddafi regime. The involvement of British Forces was very much a stop start affair, as elements were changed on various key points such as how far the UK should go. These arguments were thrashed out in a series of meetings of the National Security Council at Downing Street.

The first significant involvement of British forces in Libya was a rescue mission mounted just a couple of weeks after the Civil war broke out. On 3 March, Royal Air Force C130 aircraft were sent to a desert airstrip at Zilla in the south of the country to rescue expatriate oil workers. Many had been threatened by gunmen and bandits. The C130s were airlifting 150 foreigners, including about 20 Britons, to the Valletta airport in Malta. The C130 was accompanied by 24 members of C Squadron SBS. The C130s landed onto the desert airstrip in a large cloud of dust, as soon as they had landed, the C130s ramp was lowered and the SBS ran off the back to set up a perimeter to secure the landing site. The 150 needing to be airlifted quickly boarded the C130s before the SBS boarded and their aircraft took off without being spotted by any Libyan forces. The workers were all at very high risk of being either abducted or murdered and needed to be evacuated as quickly as possible. This small yet successful mission had been the start of Special Force operations by UK forces in Libya.

The next mission would not be quite so successful, this time E Squadron originally formed in 2005 to work with Mi6 on missions where maximum discretion is required. After 9/11, with major military commitments in Afghanistan and Iraq, MI6 stepped up its intelligence-gathering in many places that had hitherto been off the radar or considered too dangerous.

It was often backed up by UK Special Forces, but the competing demands on them to support special operations in Afghanistan and Iraq eventually led to the creation of E Squadron. E Squadron is a composite organisation formed from selected SAS, SBS and Special Reconnaissance Regiment operators. It is not technically part of the SAS or SBS, but at the disposal of the Director of Special Forces and Mi6. The squadron often operates in plain clothes and with the full range of national support, such as false identities, at its disposal.

The Secret Intelligence Service, or Mi6, sought to step up communications with some of its contacts in the opposition in Libya. It was decided to send a pair of the service's people to a town not far from Benghazi to meet one of these Libyans. The mission to Libya was to initially meet local "fixers" who would help them get to the meeting with rebel forces and see how the UK could offer support. E Squadron was tasked with looking after the two Mi6 operatives. The group of eight boarded a Chinook HC3 Special Forces helicopter for the journey to a position just outside of Bengazi in Libya.

They landed in their secret location, but almost as soon as they had landed and disembarked, they became surrounded highly suspicious farmers. The helicopters mere presence had aroused suspicion of the locals. They were equipped with a variety of weapons and secure communications gear. In keeping with E Squadron's sensitive role, they were in plain clothes, and carried a variety of passports. Witnesses stated that they were carrying weapons, ammunition, maps and passports from four different countries. Like any civil war, there was a good deal of paranoia about foreign mercenaries and spies, and the British party could not have appeared more suspicious. Especially, when they stated they were unarmed and when searched weapons were found on them. They were all detained and taken to Benghazi, the men on the ground having decided that to open fire would destroy the very bridge-building mission they were engaged in. The incident became even more of an embarrassment when the Gaddafi government released an intercepted phone call in which a British diplomat pleaded with the NTC for the team's release. They would be eventually released unharmed, but not before the damage had been done and using Special Forces to help topple the regime would be sidelined for months. It also caused great difficulties for Mi6, which had plans to turn some key figures in Gaddafi's inner circle.

On 19 March, Colonel Gaddafi's tanks were bombed as they entered Benghazi. This caused the conflict to enter a very different phase. High-profile military action was under way, and the leaders of the UK, US, and France were increasingly committed to the overthrow of the Libyan leader. Any action was tightly controlled after the bitter experience of

Iraq both in the use of UN sanctions and air action. Under UN Security Council Resolution 1973, countries were authorised to use force "to protect civilians and civilian populated areas under threat of attack". The text noted that the measures used to achieve this aim excluded "a foreign occupation force of any form on any part of Libyan territory". The authorized force meant that it had many limitations, including support to forces fighting Col Gaddafi's army and having actual UN soldiers on the ground in Libya. This did define what Britain's response would be. At Downing Street many key figures believed that airstrikes alone would not achieve the results they wanted. At various meetings of the National Security Council, Gen Richards and Mr Fox made the case for planning to provide training and equipment for the revolutionary forces of the NTC. It was towards the end of March 2011, that authorisation was given to undertake limited steps to help develop the NTC forces on the ground. This involved the immediate dispatch of a small advisory team that would help in the longer term train and equip the NTC.

When half a dozen British officers arrived at a seaside hotel in Benghazi at the beginning of April, they were unarmed and their role was very limited. They had been given orders that they were to help the NTC set up a nascent defence ministry, located in a commandeered factory on the outskirts of the city. The first and most obvious task to the advisors to get the various bands of Libyan fighters driving around in armed pickup trucks under some sort of central coordination. Most had little or no idea of what they were doing or what objectives to target. Many on seeing Colonel Gaddafi's forces would panic and quickly be outflanked - due to poor tactics and situational awareness. Many legal issues prevent further support and legal doubts were raised about arming the NTC or targeting Colonel Gaddafi.

With the air operation in full swing, these issues became even more vexed, and NATO did not want to have forces on the ground controlling the airstrikes. Although Misrata rebels used sophisticated rangefinder to adjust artillery fire and co-ordinate NATO airstrikes. The British government's desire to achieve the overthrow of Gaddafi while accommodating the legal sensitivities registered by various Whitehall departments, led to some frustration among those who were meant to make the policy work. The accidental bombing of NTC columns by NATO aircraft in early April provided those who wanted more direct assistance with a valuable argument. This allowed the British and French officers on the ground to enable a closer co-ordination to prevent further accidental bombings or clashes.

In March 2011, General Richards had started a series of low-profile visits to Doha, the capital of Qatar. Qatar had taken a leading role in backing the NTC, and its defence chief. By June 20011 it was brokering an agreement with the UK and France to provide material back-up as well as training for the NTC. France was to prove more forward-leaning than the UK in this, and by August 2001 was providing weapons to NTC units in the Nefusa Mountains of western Libya. The UK, meanwhile, had agreed to focus its efforts in the east of the country. It was as part of this new effort that British Special Forces returned to Libya. With this some members of D Squadron 22 SAS were allowed to start training and mentoring NCT units. They were in place by late August 201. The SAS operated closely with Qatar Special Forces who had reportedly delivered items such as Milan anti-tank missiles. The feelings from London was that the training should be delivered from outside Libya to remain the right side of the UN resolution. However, it was not long before the SAS were soon present at a base in southern Libya. As the war progressed The SAS strayed beyond its training facility, with single men or pairs accompanying NTC commanders that they had been training, back to their units. They dressed themselves as Libyans and blended in with the units they mentored to ensure no suspicion was aroused. As the revolutionaries fought their way into Gaddafi's home town of Sirte, they were assisted by a handful of British and other special forces. Members of the Jordanian and United Arab Emirates armies had fallen in behind the Qataris too.

On 20 October, Colonel Gaddafi was finally captured and killed by NTC men. This was followed by NATO airstrikes on a convoy of vehicles carrying, leading members of the former regime as they tried to escape from Sirte at dawn. It is quite possible British forces had a hand in coordinating this, although. In keeping with its longstanding policies on Special Forces and Mi6 operations, Whitehall has refrained from public statements about the nature of assistance on the ground. British sources agree Qatar played a leading role they put more soldiers into Libya than the UK. The suggestion is that altogether the number of soldiers committed to the ground in Libya did not exceed a couple of hundred. It is part of the essence of Special Forces of this kind that they often operate in secrecy, providing their political masters with policy options that they might not wish to own up to publicly. Given that the UK's earlier relationship with Colonel Gaddafi and his intelligence services caused great embarrassment - it could be that attention will one day focus more closely on British assistance to the NTC as the years pass or issues arise from any of the assistance given.

Glossary

ACMAT - ACMAT (Ateliers de Construction Mécanique de L'Atlantique) now owned as a subsidiary of Renault trucks, have produced military vehicles since 1958. They are known for their Known for their reliability, simplicity, ruggedness and their 80%. Over 3500 parts are interchangeable between various models. They were originally designed for and targeted at African and Asian countries who could not afford more expensive vehicles.

Airbus A300 – The A300 is a short- to medium-range wide-body jet airliner that was developed and manufactured by Airbus. Released in 1972 as the world's first twin-engined widebody airliner. It first flew on 28 October 1972 and continued in production until 2007. Powered by two CF6-50C2 or JT9D-59A engines and with a range of 3,600Nm. It could carry between 220 and 375 passengers depending on configuration.

Aérospatiale SA 330 Puma – The Puma was originally manufactured by Sud Aviation of France, and continued to be produced by Aérospatiale. It is a four bladed, twin engine medium lift helicopter. It first flew in April 1965 and is powered by two Turboméca Turmo IVC turboshafts. It has been used in a variety of conflicts and wars around the world and has also proved popular as a civilian transport helicopter.

AK47 – The AK47 Kalashnikov assault rifle more commonly known as the AK-47 or just AK (Avtomat Kalashnikova – 47, which translates to the Kalashnikov automatic rifle, model 1947), and its derivatives. It had been and still is with minor modifications, manufactured in dozens of countries, and has been used in hundreds of countries and conflicts since its introduction. The total number of the AK-type rifles made worldwide during the last 60 years is estimated at 90+ million. The AK47 is known for its simplicity of operation, ruggedness and maintenance, and unsurpassed reliability even in the most inhospitable of conditions.

Apache AH64 – The Bowing Apache AH64 is a twin engine attack helicopter with quite formidable firepower consisting of a fully movable

30mm cannon, rockets and Hellfire missiles stored in pods on the stubby wings.

Boeing 737 is a short to medium range,narrow body twin engine jet airliner. It first flew on the 9 April 1967 and went into revenue service on the 10 February 1968. The 737 series is the best-selling jet airliner in the history of aviation. The 737 has been continuously manufactured by Boeing since 1967 with 7,865 aircraft delivered. Originally powered by two Pratt & Whitney JT8D low bypass turbofan engines. It is now powered by two CFM International CFM56-7 series high bypass turbofan offering an extra 5000lbf of thrust whilst being more economical over the original JT8D.

BTR-80 is an 8x8 wheeled amphibious armoured personnel carrier (APC) designed in the USSR. Adopted in 1986 and replaced the previous versions, BTR-60 and BTR-70 in the Soviet Army. It entered service in 1986 and weighs 15 tons. Powered by a KamAZ-7403 260hp diesel, it has a top speed of 56mph. Armed with a 14.5 mm KPVT machine gun and a 7.62 mm PKT machine gun.

C8 - The C8 was born out of the C7 when in 1984; Canada adopted a new 5.56 mm assault rifle. The C7 itself was based on a later version of the M16. To avoid research and design expenses, the Canadians simply purchased the license from the USA for a new assault rifle, chambered for the latest 5.56 x 45 NATO ammunition. This was the Colt model 715, also known as the M16A1E1 rifle. Adopted as the C7, this rifle combined features from both earlier M16A1 rifles and the newest M16A2. Later on, Diemaco (now Colt Canada) developed a short-barrelled carbine version, fitted with telescoped buttstock, which was designated the C8.

CH-47 Chinook - The CH-47 Chinook is an American helicopter built by Boeing with a tandem rotor design. It first flew in September 1961 and has gone through many changes since then. Originally powered by two Lycoming T55-GA-714A turboshaft engines. It has seen service around the world with the USAF, USMC, RAF in a variety of conflicts and wars. It is currently in service with 26 different countries and a total of 1179 have been built.

DShK – The DShK is a Russian heavy machine gun that came into service in 1938. It is gas operated, with a 12.7x109 mm calibre belt fed and air-cooled machine gun. It can be used as an anti-aircraft gun mounted on a pintle. It is also easily mounted to trucks or other vehicles as an infantry heavy support weapon.

General Dynamics F-16 'Fighting Falcon' – The F-16 is a single engine supersonic, multirole fighter aircraft, developed for the USAF. It first flew in January 1974 and is powered by a single F110-GE-100 afterburning turbofan engine. It is one of the most manoeuvrable aircraft in the world and is used by the U.S. Air Force Thunderbirds display team and has been exported to quite a few air forces around the world.

Grumman F14 'Tomcat' - The Grumman F-14 Tomcat is a U.S. Navy supersonic, twin-engine, two-seat, variable-sweep wing fighter aircraft. Made famous in the film 'Top Gun,' it first flew in December 1970 and retired in September 2006. It is still being flown by the Iranian Air Force. Powered by two General Electric F110-GE-400 afterburning turbofans, it was designed to fire the long-range Aim-54 Phoenix missile. In later years, it was adapted to drop bombs to widen its mission capability.

Humvee – The HMMWV (High Mobility Multipurpose Wheeled Vehicle), commonly known as the Humvee, is an American four-wheel drive military vehicle produced by AM General. It has largely supplanted the roles formerly served by smaller Jeeps. It has been in service since 1984 and served in all theatres of war. Powered by an 8 Cylinder. Diesel 6.2 L or 6.5 L V8 turbo diesel and with a top speed of over 70 mph, which drops to 55mph when loaded up to its gross weight. It initially lacked any armour, but later version has had some armour protection added against small arms fire.

Lockheed C130 Hercules – The Lockheed C130 Hercules is a four engine turboprop transport aircraft with a high wing design. It first flew in August 1954. Since then there have been many variants used by over

70 countries around the world. Originally powered by four 4 Allison T56-A-15 turboprops. It can carry a payload of around 20,000 kg or up to 92 passengers. It is a highly versatile aircraft and has seen use across the world over its 50 years of continuous service.

Lockheed C141 - Lockheed C-141 Starlifter was used up until its retirement in 2006 as a heavy lift aircraft. It was of a high wing design with a landing ramp at the rear. It first flew in December 1963 before being replaced in 2006 by the C-17 Globemaster III. Powered by four Pratt & Whitney TF33-P-7 turbofans it could carry a max payload of up to 28,900 kg.

M4 Carbine - The M4 carbine is a family of firearms that are originally based on earlier carbine versions of the M16 rifle. The M4 is a shorter and lighter variant of the M16A2 assault rifle, allowing its user to better operate in close quarters combat. It has 80% parts commonality with the M16A2. It is a gas-operated, magazine-fed, selective fire, shoulder-fired weapon with a telescoping stock. Like the rest of the M16 family, it fires the standard .223 calibre, or 5.56mm NATO round.

M16 – The M16 is a lightweight, 5.56 mm, air-cooled, gas-operated, magazine-fed assault rifle, with a rotating bolt, actuated by direct impingement gas operation. The rifle is made of steel, 7075 aluminium alloy, composite plastics and polymer materials. It was developed from the AR-15 and came into service in 1963. The M16 is now the most commonly manufactured 5.56x45 mm rifle in the world. Currently the M16 is in service with more than 80 countries worldwide. It has grown a reputation for ruggedness and reliability and was adopted by the SAS over the less reliable SA80. Later the SAS adopted the C8.

McDonnell Douglas F15E 'Strike Eagle' – The F15E Strike Eagle is an all-weather multirole fighter, derived from the McDonnell Douglas (now Boeing) F-15 Eagle. It is powered by two Pratt & Whitney F100-229 afterburning turbofans, 29,000 lbf and capable of Mach 2.5 (2.5 the speed of sound). It first flew in December 1986 and an F15SG version is on order by the ordered by the Republic of Singapore Air Force (RSAF).

McDonnell Douglas F/A18 'Hornet' – The F/A18 is a U.S. Navy twin engine supersonic, all-weather carrier-capable multirole fighter jet, designed to be carrier based. It first flew in November 1978 and was initially powered by two General Electric F404-GE-402 turbofans. McDonnell Douglas is now Boeing after being merged in 1997.

MH/AH-6M Little Bird - The MH-6 Little Bird (nicknamed the Killer Egg), and its attack variant AH-6, are light helicopters used for special operations in the U.S. Army. It is a single engine lightweight helicopter that first flew in February 1963. Powered by one T63-A-5A or T63-A-700 turboshaft engine and with a top speed of 175 mph. In many ways made famous in sequences in the 1980s in the A Team, Air Wolf and more recently the film Black Hawk Down.

Mil Mi-8 is a Soviet-designed medium twin-turbine Transport helicopter. There are also armed gunship versions. The Mi-8 is among the world's most-produced helicopters, used by over 50 countries. Russia is the main producer and the largest operator of the Mi-8/Mi-17 helicopter. It first flew in 1961 and was used as a basis to develop the Mi-24 Hind attack helicopter. Powered by two Klimov TV3-117Mt turboshafts,1,950 hp each a top speed of 173mph and a range of 280 miles.

Mi-25 also known as the 'Hind D' is a Russian designed and built attack helicopter, gunship and troop carrier. It is a large attack helicopter and heavily armoured, it first flew in 1969 and has seen use, with a variety of armed forces across the globe. Over 2,300 have been built so far. It was developed from the Mil Mi-8 transport helicopter. It is powered by two Isotov TV3-117 turbines, 2,200hp each and a top speed of 208 mph and a range of 280 miles. The Mi-25 weighs over 8 tons empty and is 57 feet long and 21 feet high.

Northern Alliance - The Afghan Northern Alliance, officially known as the United Islamic Front for the Salvation of Afghanistan, was a military front that came to formation in late 1996 after the Islamic Emirate of Afghanistan (Taliban) took over Kabul. The United Front was assembled by key leaders of the Islamic State of Afghanistan, particularly president in exile Burhanuddin Rabbani and former Defence Minister Ahmad Shah Massoud.

RPD Light Machine Gun is an automatic weapon using a gas-operated long stroke piston system and a locking system recycled from previous Degtyaryov small arms, consisting of a pair of hinged flaps set in recesses on each side of the receiver. It fires 7.62 mm ammunition from a cylindrical metal container that clips on and holds 100 rounds. It can fire 650-750 rounds per minute an is an effective ire support weapon. For firing from the prone position, as well as adding stability when firing, a bipod is fitted to the front of the weapon.

SLR or L1A1 Self-Loading Rifle was a British derivative of the Belgian FN FAL battle rifle, produced under licence. It has seen use in the armies of Australia, Canada, India, Jamaica, Malaysia, New Zealand, Rhodesia. It was replaced by the SA80 in the 1980s. It fires a 7.62 NATO round with a 20 or 30 round magazine. The effective firing range is 1968 feet. No longer in service with the British armed forces, it is still in service around the world.
SR-25 (Stoner Rifle-25) is a semi-automatic special application sniper rifle designed by Eugene Stoner and manufactured by Knight's Armament Company. It fires 7.62mm ammunition and came into service in 1990, first being used in anger in Somalia in 1993.

Sikorsky UH-60 Black Hawk – The UH-60 Black Hawk has been cemented in history after the books and film 'Black hawk down'. It is a four bladed twin engine medium lift helicopter designed for the United States Army. It first flew in October 1974 and has been used in a variety of roles and variants since then. Powered by two General Electric T700-GE-701C turboshaft engines it can carry a variety of payloads and be adapted to suit a wide variety of missions. It was designed from the outset to a high survivability on the battlefield. First being used in combat during the invasion of Grenada in 1983.

Super Entard – The Dassault-Breguet Super Étendard is a French carrier borne strike aircraft that first flew on 28 October 1978 and has served with the French Navy, Argentine Navy and Iraqi Air Force. Powered by a single SNECMA Atar 8K-50 turbojet it has a top speed of 733mph at low level and a range of 1130 miles.

Sukhio Su-22 'Fitter' aircraft is a Soviet attack aircraft developed from the Sukhoi Su-7 fighter-bomber that first flew in 1966 and entered Russian service in 1970. It was widely exported to communist and Middle Eastern air forces as the Su-20 and Su-22, being called the Su-17 in Russia. Powered by an ingle engine and capable of Mach 1.7 at altitude. It retired from Russian service in 1998, but over 500 still fly with air forces around the world.

T-72 is a second-generation tank entering service in 1973 and went on to become the most common tank used by the Warsaw pact. Its basic design has been used in the T-90. It weighs 41 tons and has a 125 mm 2A46M smoothbore gun, 7.62 mm PKT coax machine gun and 12.7 mm NSVT antiaircraft machine gun. Powered by a V-12 diesel with 780 hp and a top speed of 37 mph. Over 25,000 have been produced so far and it currently remains in production.

Warrior Tank – The Warrior tank is lightweight tracked vehicle introduced in 1988. It is powered by a Perkins V-8 Condor Diesel engine and a top speed of 46 mph. Armament consists of a 30 mm L21A1 RARDEN cannon, although the 40 mm CTA International CT40 cannon is planned as a future upgrade. Secondary weapons are a L94A1 coaxial 7.62 mm chain gun and a 7.62 mm machine gun. The plan is to upgrade the warrior tanks further to keep them in service until 2025.

Westland Lynx – The Lynx is a British multi-purpose military helicopter that has been in service since 1978 and had its first flight in March 1971. It was the first aerobatic helicopter and still holds the helicopter speed record after being specially modified. Powered by two 2 × Rolls-Royce Gem turboshaft engines, the Lynx has proven itself as a versatile helicopter and quite potent as an attack helicopter. The latest version the Wildcat is due to enter operational service in 2014.

ZSU-23-2 – The ZU-23-2 "Sergey" is a Soviet towed 23 mm anti-aircraft twin-barrelled autocannon. It was designed to engage low-flying targets at a range of 2.5 km as well as armoured vehicles at a range of 2 km and for direct defence of troops and strategic locations against air assault usually conducted by helicopters and low-flying airplanes. Normally, once each barrel has fired 100 rounds, it becomes too hot and is therefore replaced with a spare barrel.

Short History of the SAS

1947 - May 1st - the SAS is revived in the form of 21st Battalion, Army Air Corps SAS a Territorial Army Unit.

1950 - 21 SAS deploy to the Korean War.

1950 - 1955 Malaya - 21 SAS deploy to Malaya, renamed as the 'Malayan Scouts', in response to the 'Malayan Emergency' insurrection. Much of the Regiment's expertise in jungle warfare are learnt in this period.

1952 -The SAS is reorganised into 22nd Special Air Service Regiment and 21st Special Air Service Regiment.

1958 - 1959 Oman - The SAS was deployed to the Gulf state of Oman, battling forces opposed to the Sultan.

1959 - The 23rd Special Air Service Regiment, a Territorial Army (reserve forces) unit, is created.

1963 - 1966 - Counter Insurgency, the SAS support guerrillas during the Indonesia-Malaysia confrontation in Borneo, Brunei and Sarawak

1964 - 1967 – Aden, the SAS deploy for counter-insurgency operations in the British protectorate.

1970 - 1977 - Dhofor, Oman, the SAS are sent to Oman to fight against another insurrection.

1972 - Counter Terrorism, following the intervention by German police during the Munich hostage crisis that went wrong, the SAS create the Counter-Revolutionary War wing. The CRW wing begins developing techniques for both counter-terrorism and body-guarding operations.

1972 - The QE2, when a bomb-threat is issued against the QE2, a team comprising of SAS/SBS & Army bomb disposal experts parachute into the sea, board the liner and perform a search. No bomb was found.

1975 - Stansted hijacking when the SAS's first real test of their techniques developed by the CRW wing, the SAS storm a hijacked airliner at Stansted airport. Using non-lethal force, they arrest the lone hijacker.

1975 - The Balcombe Street Siege, was when an IRA operation ends with a family being held hostage in a London flat. As the SAS prepare to intervene, news of their arrival is leaked to the media. Upon hearing this news, the IRA men promptly surrender to police. Without a bullet being fired.

1976 - The SAS deploy to Northern Ireland. In response to the worsening crisis in Northern Ireland, the SAS, who had been over the water in small numbers since 1973, mostly in advisory roles, are now deployed directly in strength to take on the IRA, following targets, gathering intelligence and take downs.

1977 - Lufthansa hijacking, when a German Airliner is hijacked by terrorists, GSG-9, the German counter-terrorist unit, receives assistance from the SAS. Two SAS soldiers accompany the GSG-9 assault team as they pursue the hijacked airliner to Mogadishu, Somalia. As the GSG-9 team stormed the cabin, the two SAS men threw stun grenades to distract the hijackers.

1980 - Operation Nimrod, B Squadron, storm the Iranian Embassy in London after twenty-six hostages are taken.

1981 - The Gambia, in August 1981, three SAS men were sent to the Gambia to assist President Jawara's regime in putting down a coup attempt by Cuban-backed Marxist rebels. Hostages taken by the rebels included members of the President's family. The three-man SAS team managed to rescue all of the hostages and help restore Jawara to power.

1982 - The Falklands the SAS play a major part in the British campaign to retake the Falkland Islands from Argentine invaders. This included gathering intelligence, acting as target spotters for the Harrier and going back to their World War Two roots blowing up aircraft on Pebble Island.

1982 -1989 – Afghanistan, following the invasion of Afghanistan by the Soviet Union in 1979, a number of SAS men were sent to advise anti-Soviet forces in Afghanistan. These men officially 'leave' the Regiment to be hired by a front company of the SIS, Britain's secret service. They are then contracted to go to Afghanistan where they link up with Afghani rebels. The SAS men lead the rebels on hit-and-run missions against Russian supply convoys. Once US-made Stinger SAMs become available, the SAS instruct the Mujahidin on their use. Some Afghanis are brought over to the UK and trained by SAS instructors.

1984 - Libyan Embassy in London In April 1984, the SAS anti-terrorist team deployed to London and stormed the Libyan embassy following the shooting of British policewoman from a shot fired within the embassy. A diplomatic solution was reached and the SAS were stood down.

1985 – Botswana, following a series of cross-border attacks by South African forces, B Squadron provide training to the Botswana Defence Force (BDF).

1987 - Peterhead Prison, in a quite controversial use of the SAS in a domestic situation, a team of SAS are sent to quell the riots at Peterhead Prison and rescue a Prison Warder being held hostage. The SAS used Batons, stun grenades and CS gas, rather than lethal force and their quick attack meant the hostage was rescued without injury to the SAS, hostage or prisoners.

1988-1989 – Beirut, the SAS deploy to Beirut to prepare the ground for a rescue of kidnapped Western hostages including Terry Waite and John McCarthy. Covert teams carry out surveillance of possible insertion/extraction sites and routes in/out but in the end the mission is called off.

1988 – Gibraltar, three suspected IRA terrorists are shot dead by the SAS on the streets of Gibraltar in the controversial 'Operation Flavius'.

1989 - 1991 – Columbia SAS teams train and assist Columbian forces in their struggle against the drug, cartels.

1991 - Gulf War A, D & part of B Squadron deploy to the Gulf in response to Saddam Hussein's invasion of Kuwait. As Iraq invades Kuwait, A British Airways passenger plane, Flight 149, stops at Kuwait International Airport in order to deliver a group of men, speculated to be SAS operatives. The action causes the plane's passengers to be detained by the Iraqis and form part of Saddam's 'human shield'. A & D squadron Land Rover columns drive far behind Iraqi lines initially on search and destroy operations, then later becoming part of efforts to find and destroy Iraqi Scud missile launchers. B Squadron insert foot patrols to watch main supply routes (MSRs) for Scud convoys. One patrol, Bravo Two Zero, are compromised and try to escape and evade to Syria.

1991 – Zaire, a small SAS team is sent to protect the British Embassy in the troubled African nation of Zaire. Whilst there, the SAS ensure that all British diplomatic staff are safely evacuated from the country.

1993 - The Waco Siege, One or two SAS soldiers are sent to advise US authorities over the siege of the Branch Davidian cult at Waco, Texas.

1994/95 - Bosnia, the SAS support the UN peacekeeping efforts in Bosnia and become caught up in the siege of Gorazde.

1995 - Sierra Leone, a two-man SAS team are sent to Sierra Leone to carry out intelligence gathering and a feasibility study for a possible rescue of westerners taken hostage by African rebels. All hostages are eventually released without need for any military intervention.

1997 - Lima, Peru, the SAS advises the Peruvian authorities on a commando raid to end a four-month siege of the Japanese embassy in Lima. One of the hostages dies in the operation, together with two Peruvian commandos and 14 hostage-takers.

1997 – Bosnia SAS teams, working under a NATO remit, arrest several suspected war criminals.

1997 – Albania, in late March, the SAS extract British Aid Worker, Robert Welch from war-torn Albania. The 4-man SAS team, in a two Land Rover convoy meet Welch at a prearranged point then drive him to a helicopter landing zone. Two Chinooks land and a security force made up of troops from The Prince of Wales Royal Regiment debussed and fanned out around the landing zone. The two SAS Land Rovers, including Welch, are driven up into the Chinook's cargo hold and shortly after the rescue force is airborne, flying low across the Albanian countryside and out to sea for a refuelling stop on an American Aircraft Carrier stationed in the Adriatic.

A day later, a British couple, Mike and Judy Smith, were safely escorted to safety by the SAS. The Smiths were running an orphanage in Elbasan, in the Albania countryside and had phoned the British embassy in the capital, Tirana, when a series of gang-related killings cause them to fear for the children in their care. An SAS convoy of 3 vehicles drive to the orphanage and set up secure satellite communications. The British couple are given 30 minutes to prepare themselves and the 22 children to move. As the convoy drives towards the relative safety of Tirana, 2 RAF Chinooks escort them, ready to land and evacuate the passengers if needed. The SAS, with the British couple and children arrive in Tirana without incident.

1998 - The Gulf, a small number of SAS and SBS forces are deployed to the Persian Gulf to act as Combat Search and Rescue (CSAR) forces for downed allied air crew during the US-led bombing of Iraqi targets in the second Gulf war.

1999 – Kosovo, the SAS play a part in the NATO intervention against the Serbian action in Kosovo

2000 - An Afghani Boeing 727 airliner is hijacked and flown to Stansted Airport in February 2000. The SAS anti-terrorist team deploys and prepares to storm the plane if necessary. The drama comes to a peaceful end as it emerges that the hijack was an immigration ploy by some of the passengers.

2000 - Sierra Leone Summer 2000: SAS patrols carry out fact-finding missions in support of the UN mission in the war-torn African nation. May 23 - A small SAS team secure RUF leader Foday Sankoh during violent clashes in the Capital, Freetown. Sankoh is spirited away to British custody.

June 15 - SAS spotters on the ground help to guide Indian and British helicopters in rescuing more than 200 UN observers and soldiers held hostage by Revolutionary United Front rebels. (Operation Khukri) September 2000: When British Soldiers are held hostage by rebels, the SAS lead a daring rescue mission to free them. The was a joint mission with the PARA's

2001 – Macedonia, the SAS deploy to Macedonia as part of efforts to prevent another large-scale Balkans conflict.

2001 – Afghanistan, in the aftermath of the terrorist attacks of September 11th, the SAS deploy to Afghanistan and undertake reconnaissance missions along with operations to capture key Taliban figures. The SAS also carried out a large-scale assault on an opium processing plant doubling as a Taliban/Al-Qaeda base in 'Operation Trent'.

2003 to date – Iraq The SAS played a role in the US-led invasion of Iraq although the precise details of their involvement are not publicly known as yet. They supported America Delta Force and SEAL teams in a variety of missions. Following the initial invasion, the SAS work with TF-121 (now TF-88), and a US-led team of Special Operations units tasked with hunting down high-value members of Saddam's regime as well as targeting Al-Qaeda. The SAS commit a full Squadron to 'Task Force Black'.

2004 - October - The SAS is put on standby to rescue kidnapped British citizen, Ken Bigley who is later killed by his captors.

2005 - July - A 16-man SAS sniper team kill three suicide bombers as they leave their house in Baghdad.

2005 - 19th September - The SAS rescue 2 SRR operatives who had been held by Iraqi police with alleged links to the insurgency.

2006 - 23rd March - Members of B Squadron, SAS, rescue British peace activist, Norman Kmber + 2 Canadians from their kidnappers in Baghdad.

2004 - Testing Security at GCHQ, A joint SAS/SBS team infiltrate GCHQ, Britain's communications intelligence headquarters as a part of a security exercise.

2005 - The Olympics, the SAS, along with the SBS, are sent to Greece to advise the Greek authorities and to protect visiting British dignitaries against the threat of terrorism.

2005 - July bombings, following 2 waves of terrorist attacks in London, UK Special Forces, including the SAS, SBS and SRR deploy on the streets of British cities, assessing security weak points and providing rapid-response support to police operations. SAS troopers, skilled in explosive entry, assist the Met Armed Response unit, C019, in arresting suspected terrorists.

2007 – Somalia, the SAS reportedly deploy to Somalia in January, tracking down Al-Qaeda members fleeing from US airstrikes.

2007 – London 22 January - An SAS unit is reportedly permanently deployed to London in order to assist the Police in counter terrorist operations

2007 – Ethiopia March 7 - The SAS is put on standby to intervene in the kidnapping of Britons in Ethiopia.

2007 – Baghdad, September - The SAS joins the hunt for an Al-Qaeda killer operating in Baghdad.

2011 – SAS and MI6 operatives were captured by the Libyan rebels and had their weapons taken; they were later released.

2012 – Afghanistan, the SAS along with U.S SEALs launch a rescue mission of four hostages including a British citizen, Helen Johnston. Five Taliban fighters were killed during the rescue mission.

Short History of Delta Force

Delta is relatively young compared to the SAS, SBS and Navy SEALs, having been formed in 1977 by its first commander. Colonel Charles Beckwith was tasked to form the new unit and pulled largely from the Special Forces Groups. The type of missions the SFOD-Delta has been involved with over the past few decades are classified but some have been de-classified. Here is a list of several of the declassified engagements up to the present day:

1980 Operation Eagle Claw - During the Iran Hostage Crisis a failed attempt at a rescue due to aviation equipment/operator error led to the death of eight Americans; as a result, the 160th Special Operations Aviation Regiment was created.

1983 Operation Urgent Fury - Grenada prisoner rescue from the Richmond Hill prison.

1989 Operation Just Cause - Panama invasion to capture Noriega and protect some 35,000 Americans living in Panama.

1991 Gulf War - Iraq invades Kuwait and the US-led alliance defeats Saddam Hussein and his Army, pushing them back into Iraq.

1993 Operation Gothic Serpent - Part of the Battle of Mogadishu, where U.S. helicopters were shot down and two Delta Operators SFC Randall Shughart and MSG Gary Gordon were awarded the Congressional Medal of Honor for their efforts that day.

2001 War in Afghanistan -Within a month of the September 11, 2001 attacks, Special Forces operators aided in defeating and dismantling the Taliban in Afghanistan.

2001 Battle of Tora Bora - A massive joint engagement to kill or capture Osama bin Laden.

2003 Operation Red Dawn - Locating and capturing Saddam Hussein.

Countless Hostage Rescues around the world

Short History of the U.S. Navy SEALs

1941: Training began for units referred to as Amphibious Scouts and Raiders.

1943: The first group of volunteers selected from the Naval Construction Battalions (Seabees).

1947: The Navy organized its first underwater offensive strike units.

1950 June – 1953 June: During the Korean Conflict, these Underwater Demolition Teams (UDTs) took part in the landing at Inchon as well as other missions including demolition raids on bridges and tunnels accessible from the water.

1960s: Each branch of the armed forces formed its own counterinsurgency force. The Navy used UDT personnel to form units called SEAL teams.

1961, May 25: President John F. Kennedy speaks before the U.S. Congress authorizing the establishment of the Navy SEALs.

1961 Navy SEALs are officially approved for operations via the Chief of Naval Operations Admiral Arleigh Burke.

1962 January 1, 1pm: SEAL Team ONE was commissioned in the Pacific Fleet and SEAL Team TWO in the Atlantic Fleet. These teams were developed to conduct unconventional warfare, counter-guerrilla warfare and clandestine operations.

1963: First Vietnam War-detachment of elements of SEAL Team One in Da Nang, Vietnam to serve under the command of the CIA Chief of Station.

1964: SEALs became a component of the Commander-in-Chief (CINC) of Vietnams theatre forces.

1967: The Naval Operations Support Groups were renamed Naval Special Warfare Groups (NSWGs) as involvement increased in special operations.

1983: Existing UDTs were renamed as SEAL teams or SEAL Delivery Vehicle Teams and the requirement for hydrographic reconnaissance and underwater demolition became SEAL missions.

1987: SEAL team SIX became DEVGRU (DEVelopment GRoUp).

1987 April: The Naval Special Warfare Command was commissioned at the Naval Amphibious Base Coronado in San Diego, California. Its mission is to prepare Naval Special Warfare forces to carry out their assigned missions and to develop special operations strategy, doctrine, and tactics.

2001 War in Afghanistan Operation Enduring Freedom

2002 March; Operation Anaconda in the U.S. invasion of Afghanistan.

2002; (Operation Enduring Freedom-Philippines) -Captured/Killed key ASG Terrorist leader.

2003 March; participated in the 2003 invasion of Iraq and subsequent missions to capture key Iraqi personnel.

2011 Operation Neptune Spear, the capture of Osma bin Laden in Abbottabad Pakistan

Bibliography

Andy Mcnab Bravo Two Zero (Bantam press 1994)

Andy Mcnab Seven Troop (Corgi 2009)

Barry Davis Heroes f The SAS: True Stories of The British Army's Elite Special Forces Regiment (Virgin Books; New Ed edition 2007)

Chris Ryan The One That Got Away (Red Fox; Junior Ed edition 2010)

Damien Lewis Bloody Heros (Arrow; New Ed edition 2007)

Damien Lewis Zero Six Bravo: 60 Special Forces. 100,000 Enemy. The Explosive True Story (Quercus 2013)

John parker SBS: The Inside Story of the Special Boat Service (Headline; 2nd Revised edition edition 2004)

Jon Cooksey Pebble Island (Elite Forces Operations Series) (Pen & Sword Military; 2007)

Mark Nicol Ultimate Risk (Macmillan 2003)

Mark Urban Task Force Black (Abacus 2010)

Micahel Ahser The Regiment: The Real Story of the SAS (Penguin 2008)

Peter Crossland Victor Two Inside Iraq (Bloomsbury books 1996)

Peter Scholey The Joker: 20 Years Inside the SAS (Andre Deutsch Ltd; New edition edition 2007)

Peter Winner Soldier 'I': the Story of an SAS Hero: From Mirbat to the Iranian Embassy Siege and Beyond (Osprey Publishing 2010)

Steve Stone SAS Operations in Afghanistan (Digital Dreams Publishing 2013)

Sean Naylor Not a Good Day to Die (Penguin 2005)

Internet

www.USNavySEALs.Com

Printed in Great Britain
by Amazon

86288633R00108